Table of Contents

Welcome!

An Introduction from Alley Cat Allies' President and Founder

If you call out "25 years ago..." in our office halls, you'll hear everyone chime in, "...in an alley in Adams Morgan!"

Alley Cat Allies was launched as a result of my accidental shortcut down a Washington, D.C., neighborhood alleyway on July 7, 1990, where a colony of feral cats was living and co-existing with the residents.

The past is personal. We've been around for a generation now. But the past still feels close enough to touch, and it inspires us every day. From this accidental discovery, we've sparked a successful and effective movement that has changed society for cats — no matter on which side of the door they live.

Although we're called Alley Cat Allies, it's never been just about alley cats. We champion all cats — community, house, stray, feral, and each cat in between. In 1990, cats needed a voice. Over the past 25 years, we've given it to them. And we will always be their voice. We proudly use the First Amendment of our Bill of Rights in the U.S. Constitution to petition our government for a redress of grievances on behalf of cats!

Alley Cat Allies is an advocacy organization, and our mission is to educate and help communities protect and improve the lives of cats. We're a loudly purring engine for social change. We were the first organization to introduce and advocate for humane methods of community (i.e., feral) cat care in the American animal protection community.

Following the success of proven programs and published materials from the Trap-Neuter-Return (TNR) pioneers in the United Kingdom, we have mobilized compassionate people in every state. Our hands-on expertise is what sets us apart from more traditional advocacy organizations. We change policy AND we help people help cats in backyards and alleyways. We are unique in that we focus on the big picture but never lose sight of the individual cats and kittens and their colonies.

We devised guidelines for hands-on cat care for individuals and professionals, including veterinarians. Our detailed website, free booklets, brochures,

webinars, and videos have become lifelines for caregivers, activists, shelter volunteers and directors, and veterinarians.

Once considered a radical approach, today TNR is mainstream and is practiced in hundreds of communities, by thousands of veterinarians, and even in shelters (where it's sometimes called Shelter-Neuter-Return or Return to Field). Hundreds of communities and the states of Connecticut, Delaware, and Utah, plus the District of Columbia, have passed laws promoting and adopting TNR.

Many cat advocates have had their own "alley moment" — the time their eyes opened to the needs of outdoor cats. That's why we're here; the cats still need us. Millions of cats are still killed in shelters even though there are sound and humane programs to save them. We

Alley Cat Allies was launched as a result of my accidental shortcut down a Washington, D.C., neighborhood alleyway on July 7, 1990, where a colony of feral cats was living and co-existing with the residents.

intend to reach every shelter in every community (there are nearly 5,000!), which is why we still need you.

Alley Cat Allies is growing from being the leading cat protection organization in the U.S. to making an even larger positive impact throughout the world via our website and social media. We're in touch with, and helping to increase the number of, cat caregivers throughout the world. Our annual National Feral Cat Day campaign and Feral Friends Network include participants from 20 countries. We're creating alliances with local governments and leaders in "animal control" (what is becoming known as "animal care services"). We're designing cutting-edge, efficient, life-saving models.

Our 25th anniversary is the right time to pause and

lives of cats. Thank you!

This is just the beginning. This anniversary book is a selected representation of just some of our actions to celebrate two and a half decades of compassionate action for cats. To learn more about our work, please visit our website at www.alleycat.org.

Please join us as we move forward into the next quarter century of cat advocacy!

For the cats,

Becky Robinson

Becky Robinson
President and Founder

look at where we've been, where we are, and what next we need to do to protect cats.

Alley Cat Allies has evolved and will continue to do so. Our original programs continue to make a difference every day. Our hands-on work is supported by research, and our law and policy white papers are changing elected officials' decisions about animal sheltering. We are stopping bureaucratic threats to cats while working with the grassroots and advancing the public's interest in protecting cats. But we must continue to dispel myths and deepen our understanding about cats.

Cats are found the world over, and we are learning more about the domestic cat as research increases. Recent genetic and archaeological findings hint that wild cats became house cats earlier and in a different place than previously thought. It was commonly believed cats were domesticated 4,000 years ago in Egypt, but recent discoveries suggest that cat domestication began in parts of the Middle East and north Africa earlier. In the words of one of the scientists from the project, Carlos A. Driscoll, "We think what happened is that cats sort of domesticated themselves." The story of the cat is much different from that of the dog and other domesticated animals, which has informed the evolution of their treatment in society.

We're witnessing an increase in positive attitudes toward cats, but entrenched, cruel, and outdated practices (and not least ignorance) are still their enemy. We must challenge the myths and superstitions that stop cats from being protected and understood.

In the past 25 years, I think we've created a century's worth of change. I want to congratulate everyone on your commitment and what you've done to improve the

A Personal Thank You

There are thousands of people to thank for their personal contributions to Alley Cat Allies and the movement to protect cats. That is the good news. People have made the movement what it is today. The roster of names would fill another book.

Board members since the time we formed. Volunteers who have devoted evenings and weekends to spay/neuter clinics and campaigns. Veterinarians who gave their time and opened their private hospitals to caregivers. Caregivers — unsung heroes — who spent their nights trapping cats and developing new equipment and more efficient trapping protocols. Donors who have been steadfast supporters.

I want to personally thank Donna Wilcox, our chair, who has served in practically every capacity, from the Adams Morgan alley caregiver to the chair of the board! I want to thank Laura Guimond, a great friend who helped craft Alley Cat Allies' first logo and wrote our first fundraising appeal. And Bonney Brown, who attended our first conference and is a force to be reckoned with when it comes to saving animals' lives with sustainable shelter transformation.

Thank you to my family, especially my husband, Ed Lytwak. There are no words to describe his unwavering support of me, and therefore Alley Cat Allies, and his commitment to the many animals we have fostered and recovered in our home over the years. By far, the greatest influence I had growing up in Kansas was from my aunt, Mary Ann Robinson, who opened my eyes and heart to the needs of animals and people.

Becky Robinson at home with Thom.

TIMELINE

Timeline

Celebrating 25 Years of Saving Cats

1990
After discovering and helping a feral cat colony in an alleyway in the Adams Morgan neighborhood of Washington, D.C., the founders are inspired to start Alley Cat Allies. (See Achievement 1: How It All Began — Our First Alley Cat Colony)

Ellen Perry Berkeley's article "Feral Cats" in the July issue of *Cat Fancy* magazine records the early days of TNR and of the groundbreaking work of longtime ACA friend AnnaBell Washburn. Five years earlier, Ellen wrote about two TNR projects in London for *Cat Fancy*.

1991
ACA establishes the Feral Friends Network to connect Americans with local help for humane cat care, so caregivers who often felt isolated could receive support and assistance. Today, our Feral Friends Network includes thousands of experienced caregivers, veterinarians, organizations, and spay/ neuter clinics. (See Achievement 2: Feral Cats Need Allies — Making Connections with Our Feral Friends Network)

ACA publishes a case study on the successful and effective TNR of the Adams Morgan cat colony in Washington, D.C.

ACA presents at a New Jersey statewide animal rights conference where "The Control of Feral Cats" video by the Universities Federation for Animal Welfare is shown and becomes a vital humane education tool for U.S.-based activists. (See Achievement 3: Challenging the Killing: Traveling America Teaching TNR)

1992
San Francisco SPCA launches a TNR program under the direction of Rich Avanzino with ACA guidance and factsheets.

ACA conducts the first national survey researching the practice of TNR by caregivers, organizations, and shelters, and measuring public awareness and acceptance of TNR.

ACA reports the results of 14 years of TNR in the U.K. from 1977, when the Cat Action Trust was founded, through 1991. Dr. Jenny Remfry, a TNR pioneer and a veterinarian consultant to the World Society for the Protection of Animals in the U.K., wrote that the effort resulted in 22,000 cats being assisted.

ACA publishes a series of factsheets and guidelines for caregivers and veterinarians on the proper steps for TNR, plus veterinary protocols for safe handling in spay/neuter clinics and hospitals.

Comedian Kevin Nealon joins ACA as a celebrity supporter.

1993
ACA's TNR guidelines reach more than 4,000 humane societies and shelters.

ACA collaborates with and tracks the progress of large metropolitan TNR programs on the west coast, including San Diego (Feral Cat Coalition), Los Angeles (Feral Cat Committee), and San Francisco (SF SPCA, Streetcat Rescue Team, Friends of the Feral Cats, and Pets & Pals).

1994

ACA launches a low-cost clinic exclusively for cats in Washington, D.C., on two Sundays a month in cooperation with Dr. Darby Thornburgh, owner of Petworth Animal Hospital. ACA trained the new local grassroots group, Metro Ferals, to manage the program after two years. ACA recognizes Dr. Thornburgh, Charlene Thornburgh, and Sharon Lawson, for their dedication and pioneering work in TNR.

ACA brings together feral cat experts and enthusiasts from all over the country and abroad to Washington, D.C., for Focus on Ferals, the first feral cat conference held in America. Speakers include wildlife biologist Roger Tabor and veterinarian Jenny Remfry, leading international scientific authorities, who talk about the biology of cats and the benefits of TNR. (See Achievement 4: Coming Together for Cats — National Seminars Grow a Movement for Cat Protection)

1995

The first local TNR ordinances are passed and major city shelters begin practicing TNR. (See Achievement 5: Trap-Neuter-Return Ordinances — The Future of Animal Control)

Launch of Hotline, which becomes the National Cat Help Desk in 2012. (See Achievement 6 — Hotline for Cats! — National Cat Help Desk Answers the Calls)

1996

ACA submits position statement on TNR and attends the first scientific panel in the U.S., "A Critical Evaluation of Free-Roaming/Unowned/Feral Cats in the United States," convened by the American Humane Association and the Cat Fanciers' Association in Denver, Colorado. The panel reviews position papers and publishes proceedings with recommendations. CFA's Joan Miller helped to convene the landmark gathering. The seven-member panel is made up of Ph.D.s and D.V.M.s, including Margaret Slater, who later publishes research on feral cats and TNR, including "Community Approaches to Feral Cats: Problems, Alternatives, and Recommendations" (Humane Society Press, 2002).

1997

ACA's first employee, Karen Johnson, starts working in the non-air-conditioned attic of Becky Robinson's home in Arlington, Virginia.

1998

From its origins in 1994 as a Sundays-only clinic, ACA launches and finances a free, monthly clinic in Northern Virginia serving community cats in the entire Washington, D.C., region. More than 6,500 cats are cared for over the next 10 years under the direction of veterinarian Dr. Alison Mocko. (See Achievement 7: Community Cat Health Care — Our First Free Monthly Spay/Neuter Clinic)

ACA's first office opens in the Adams Morgan neighborhood of Washington, D.C., near the site of the feral cat colony that inspired ACA's founding. The headquarters and newly formed team of paid staff, funded by the generosity of ACA's supporters, is the organization's first growth spurt.

ACA introduces humane cat care to the people on the front lines of the shelter system by addressing animal control audiences. Becky Robinson is invited to speak at the first discussion of nonlethal feral cat control at a National Animal Control Association training conference. Her participation demonstrates both the growing momentum behind TNR and ACA's role as TNR experts.

ACA promotes new veterinary research from Dr. Julie Levy showing that feral cats are just as healthy as pet cats and that their feline virus (FeLV and FIV) rates are equally low. ACA starts promoting new veterinary protocol for feral cats – the removal of routine testing – that had been resulting in cats being unnecessarily killed. As a result, thousands of healthy cats are saved.

ACA holds Focus on Ferals Seminar in Pittsburgh, Pennsylvania, and offers special training for veterinarians to learn TNR of feral cats, eartipping protocol, and juvenile spay/neuter.

1999

ACA continues to promote TNR for feral cats throughout the U.S. by attending conferences, presenting workshops, and distributing materials. Initially met with resistance from established animal control and animal protection groups, and even occasionally shunned from conferences for our "radical" ideas, the backlash backfires and more attention is attracted to our nonlethal solutions.

TIMELINE

2000

When Atlantic City's animal control begins trapping and killing cats living under the city's famous boardwalk, ACA intervenes and convinces the public health director, Ron Cash, to endorse a pilot TNR program. Now called the Atlantic City Boardwalk Cats Project, the model program is still going strong and receives outspoken support from the city government, local businesses, and the community. (See Achievement 8: Cats Under the Boardwalk — Atlantic City Stops Killing and Adopts TNR)

Stopping a catch-and-kill plan, ACA becomes the first group to have a TNR contract with the U.S. military when TNR becomes an officially funded program at the Norfolk Naval Shipyard in Virginia. (See Achievement 9: U.S. Military Makes It Official — TNR Makes Rank at U.S. Naval Shipyard)

ACA launches our Cats on Campus program after hearing from students, employees, and faculty on college campuses across the country. The program recognizes the unique needs of community cat groups working at educational institutions. At the program's core is the Campus Cats listserv, where groups network and connect, share experiences and knowledge, and provide support. Today the program encompasses institutions from Stanford University to Texas A&M University. (See Achievement 10: Cats on Campus — TNR Gets Good Grades)

2001

In honor of the 10th anniversary of ACA's incorporation, we designate October 16 as National Feral Cat Day. National Feral Cat Day is a special opportunity to raise awareness about cats, promote TNR, and recognize the millions of compassionate Americans who care for outdoor cats. The campaign grows every year! (See Achievement 11: National Feral Cat Day — A Call to Action for Saving Cats)

In order to mobilize the growing number of cat lovers and advocates to take action on critical campaigns, ACA's "FeralPower! Action Center" is launched by sending e-alerts to thousands.

2002

Becky Robinson presents TNR to a global audience at the Fifth International Companion Animal Welfare Conference in Prague, the capital of the Czech Republic. *Cat Fancy* magazine lists Alley Cat Allies as one of 10 outstanding organizations.

2003

ACA sues the Florida Fish and Wildlife Conservation Commission after it adopts a policy banning TNR and endorsing the killing of cats. Although the suit is ultimately dismissed, the judge rules the policy not to be an enforceable law. Thousands of feral cats' lives are saved and caregivers in Florida continue to look after cats unhindered. (See Achievement 12: Feral Cats Take the Stand — Our Lawsuit Saves Lives)

2004

ACA establishes a pilot TNR program – DC Cat Assistance Team (DC CAT) – with the District of Columbia Department of Health, the Washington Humane Society, and the Washington Animal Rescue League, leading to a paradigm shift in community cat protection in Washington, D.C., by 2006.

2005

Soon after Hurricane Katrina, ACA opens an emergency shelter and volunteer base camp in Bogalusa, Louisiana, about 80 miles north of New Orleans. Volunteers rescue 361 cats and aid hundreds more in Louisiana and Mississippi. (See Achievement 13: Turning Tragedy into Triumph — Learning from Hurricane Katrina)

ACA and the DC Cat Assistance Team (DC CAT), in conjunction with the District of Columbia Department of Health, sponsor Feline Frenzyl, a spay/neuter clinic, and sterilizes and vaccinates 525 tame, stray, and feral cats in just two days. Colony locations were strategically selected to maximize impacts of ceasing reproduction of cats in targeted wards in the District. This was a first-of-its-kind event for the nation's capital, and may be the largest two-day clinic anywhere at the time. Humane Alliance of Asheville, North Carolina, provided veterinarians and veterinary technicians who were key to the clinic's success.

2006

After working with ACA in Washington, D.C., for two years on targeted local cat colonies stabilized by TNR campaigns, the Washington Humane Society announces it will embrace TNR for the entire community cat population in the District. Monthly subsidized spay/neuter clinics for feral cats are established. By 2008, the city passes a law requiring animal control to promote TNR for community cats. This law is now considered a model. (See Achievement 14: Leading the Way — Nation's Capital Embraces Feral Cats and TNR)

The DC CAT pilot program achieves its first goal. The District of Columbia animal services (the Washington Humane Society) launches its new TNR-based Cat Neighborhood Partnership Program (CatNiPP).

2007

ACA publishes an editorial challenging the animal control and shelter system's killing of cats as "antiquated" and far from being a "necessary evil." (See Achievement 15: Nothing "Necessary" About This Evil — The Beginning of a Much-Needed Paradigm Shift)

Alley Cat Allies becomes founding partner of the Washington Humane Society's new veterinary clinic called National Capital Area Spay & Neuter Center.

ACA launches our Every Kitty – Every City Program in five targeted metropolitan areas: Baltimore, New Orleans, Chicago, Washington, D.C., and Atlantic City. The program raises awareness about low-cost neuter services and builds local networks and support for TNR and community cat care through education, outreach, and organizing. (See Achievement 16: Every Kitty — Every City — Community-Based, Life-Saving Programs)

ACA partners with local groups to form the Spay/Neuter Coalition for a Litter-less Baltimore to improve life for cats there. The coalition revises an ordinance that prevented care for feral cats so that residents can legally care for colonies and carry out TNR. The coalition also establishes monthly seminars; educates local veterinarians on high-volume, low-cost spay/neuter techniques; and works with local animal control officers to provide resources and address concerns.

ACA introduces "Frank the Feral" mascot, who attends events, conferences, and much more!

2008

ACA launches its social media campaign with 208 Facebook friends and 11 Twitter followers. We now have more than 400,000 Facebook fans and 21,000 Twitter followers! Through our online communities, we can take even swifter action to mobilize our network to protest threats to cats as soon as harmful programs or policies are announced. But our online presence is not all business. Our office cats appear every Friday in our extremely popular LOL Cats feature. (See Achievement 17: Clicking the Mouse — Our Online Communities Connect Thousands)

The District of Columbia passes a new ordinance committing the Animal Care and Control Agency to promote the reduction of euthanasia of animals for which medical treatment or adoption is possible; and the utilization of TNR practices as a means of controlling the feral cat population, with the proviso

TIMELINE

that all efforts shall be made to adopt out trapped, tamable kittens.

After a gated community in Northern Virginia planned to trap and kill a colony of cats who were part of a TNR program, ACA rallies more than 2,000 local supporters and convinces the management to spare the cats' lives and adopt a plan that addresses residents' concerns by spaying and neutering all cats, providing community relations and humane education.

2009

ACA conducts a nationally representative study that is published as peer-reviewed scientific article in the *Journal of the American Veterinary Medical Association*. The study, "Population characteristics and neuter status of cats living in households in the United States," (K. Chu, W. M. Anderson, M. Y. Rieser) finds that family income was the single strongest predictor of whether pet cats living in households are neutered. Over 90 percent of cats in households earning $35,000 or more per year were neutered, compared to 51 percent of cats in households earning less than $35,000. (See Achievement 18: Positive Findings — Most Pet Cats Neutered)

ACA's Veterinary Awareness Campaign delivers the research, expertise, and protocols developed over 20 years to the veterinary community, which is often the first place people turn with questions about cats. ACA staff travel to veterinary conferences across the country, handing out information and promoting our online Veterinary Resource Center. (See Achievement 19: Vets are Vital — Working with Veterinarians Helps Community Cats)

2010

After a campaign led by the local cat organization Pitter Patter Paws, in conjunction with Alley Cat Allies, the New York town of Brookhaven unanimously rejects a feeding ban proposal from the town's Feral Cat Committee and instructs them to seek the advice of animal protection experts — including Alley Cat Allies — before crafting another. It is also agreed for Alley Cat Allies to provide research and information to help the committee make the right plan for Brookhaven's cats.

2011

Our 20th Anniversary celebrates two decades of advocating, educating, campaigning, and demonstrating the humane treatment of stray and feral cats in America.

"NBC Nightly News" reports on TNR and interviews ACA President Becky Robinson and community cat caregivers in Washington, D.C.

Becky Robinson is interviewed by correspondent Aasif Mandvi on "The Daily Show with Jon Stewart" on Comedy Central television.

2012

More and more people celebrate National Feral Cat Day each year. In 2012, 450 events were held nationally, with some held internationally.

The first of its kind, Alley Cat Allies launches the National Cat Help Desk and provides one-on-one assistance and a caring, supportive ear for people all across the country, handling 600 inquiries during the first month.

Alley Cat Allies President Becky Robinson testified as an expert witness on feral cats in a Virginia Circuit Court case that was later decided in favor of a caregiver feeding and neutering cats in her zoned neighborhood.

2013

Our national Architects of Change for Cats conference in Arlington, Virginia, attracts more than 350 attendees and brings together for the first time animal control, public health, police, lawyers, advocates, and veterinarians. Far surpassing our expectations, this conference catapults many new programs and initiatives in dozens of communities around the country. (See Achievement 20: A Conference of Cats — Architects of Change National Gathering)

ACA commissions our own analysis to investigate the accuracy of research about hyped data about cats and wildlife, and found that it was essentially a literature review (and not a very good one at that). (See Achievement 21: Setting the Record Straight: Challenging Dubious Research and Misinformed Media)

ACA publishes new research, "Trap-Neuter-Return Ordinances and Policies in the United States: The Future of Animal Control," a Law & Policy Brief that reports that the number of local governments with policies favoring TNR for outdoor cats has risen tenfold over the past decade, from just 23 in 2003 to 240 in 2013. The research continues into 2014 and update is published.

ACA receives the New Zealand Companion Animal Council's Assisi Award in recognition of our outstanding service to animals. For the first time, the award is presented to an organization instead of an individual. (See Achievement 22: Alley Cat Allies Recognized — Awards Means Rewards for Cats)

2014

ACA launches the Future Five: Shelter Partners to Save Cats' Lives program to help five animal shelters that reflect a cross section of sheltering in the U.S. The shelters commit to an official Feral Cat Protection Policy that ends impoundment of community cats and instead supports TNR, only accepting feral cats to divert them to TNR or Shelter-Neuter-Return programs. (See Achievement 23: The Future Five — A New Strategy for Cats in Shelters)

2015

In just six weeks of campaigning and lobbying, ACA changes the policy in Gainesville, Texas, from a cat feeding ban that sent a caregiver to jail to a supportive TNR ordinance and spay/neuter clinic.

ACA assists in nine new TNR ordinances including Rockville, Maryland; Cheyenne, Wyoming; Richland and Crocker, Missouri; Lake County, Florida; and Dunbar, West Virginia.

ACA helps Bryan, Texas, adopt a TNR ordinance, bringing the total number of TNR ordinances and policies in the U.S. to 523. This reflects the results of our national survey that showed 81 percent of Americans do not agree with the operating policy of shelters that ends more cats' lives than any other documented cause of death. The exponential growth of new humane laws is testimony to America's response to ACA's call for action to substantially reform the nation's animal control and shelter system. (See Achievement 24: Popular with the People — Humane Government Programs Wanted)

Today, more than 500,000 supporters look to Alley Cat Allies for leadership in the movement to protect cats' lives. We promote progressive policies for cats in communities all over America, and we work toward a world that values the lives of all animals.

How It All Began

Our First Alley Cat Colony

Our story began when Becky Robinson accidentally encountered a colony of feral cats (also called community cats) in an alleyway in the Adams Morgan neighborhood of Washington, D.C., one fateful summer night in 1990. In the coming weeks and months, with Louise Holton and a small group of caregivers, they figured out how to help the group of 54 cats, which eventually (naturally and humanely) declined to zero as a result of Trap-Neuter-Return (TNR).

Caregivers and newly recruited volunteers implemented TNR for the colony, taming kittens and placing them in adoptive homes, and returning adult cats back to the colony after they were spayed/neutered and vaccinated. In addition to stabilizing the population, spaying/neutering the cats ended behaviors associated with mating, including fighting and roaming, thereby making the cats less noticeable. The health of the cats also improved. By November 1997, just seven years after the TNR started, only six cats remained in the alley. The last cat from the colony died in 2007 at age 17. The original colony included Daddy Penguin, Blackie, Gremlin, Sugar Bear, Randy, and Jack.

The colony and our fledgling TNR grassroots initiative caught the attention of the media. We were

even on CNN for an entire weekend!

Louise, drawing from her experiences in South Africa where she had lived, used TNR as a method of controlling the feral cat population without killing or harming them. Few local people had heard about TNR, but an informal network of cat caretakers soon began and Alley Cat Allies was born. In 2000 Louise left ACA, leaving Becky as the director and president.

When ACA was founded, there were only a few local groups carrying out TNR. Most organizations,

Becky Robinson and AnnaBell Washburn. *Credit: Jeff Lenard.*

Below and opposite. **The Washington, D.C., feral cats who inspired Alley Cat Allies.** *Credit: Nancy Brigulio.*

even the most well-known national groups, didn't work on behalf of feral cats. But ACA began to lead a new movement that would change everything. These days, nearly all of the leading animal organizations support TNR, and hundreds of communities embrace TNR as policy. Since 1990, more than 600 nonprofits have formed on behalf of feral cats and to promote TNR. There are now countless Good Samaritans actively participating in local programs. We see striking evidence of this success everywhere we look.

Feral cats were regularly rounded up by animal control and killed in virtually every shelter and pound in the U.S. We have come a long way and saved many lives. We have changed many shelters and local laws on feral cats. But not every community has yet embraced TNR and its lifesaving program.

Also in the summer of 1990, *Cat Fancy* magazine published a groundbreaking article by Ellen Perry Berkeley about feral cats. It recorded the early days of TNR and the pioneering work of AnnaBell Washburn. AnnaBell learned about TNR from a talk given by Peter Neville, who had worked with veterinarian Dr. Jenny Remfry at the Universities Federation for Animal Welfare in the U.K.

AnnaBell became a champion of TNR in the U.S. by successfully managing feral cat colonies on Martha's Vineyard with her organization, the Pet Adoption and Welfare Service. AnnaBell and her husband, Stan, who worked for PanAm, went to London to pick up

squeeze traps to use for their TNR work. They worked with Dr. Jim Ross from the veterinary school at Tufts University and set up a TNR program on the Virgin Gorda Islands in the British Virgin Islands. AnnaBell

The original colony included Daddy Penguin, Blackie, Gremlin, Sugar Bear, Randy, and Jack.

and Stan did the trapping; Tufts students performed the spay/neuter surgeries. In a typical summer, 50-100 cats were treated. AnnaBell became a longtime ACA friend, and our work for cats continues to be inspired by her commitment and enthusiasm.

In 2004, ACA published *TNR Past, Present and Future: A History of the Trap-Neuter-Return Movement*, by Ellen Perry Berkeley. Ellen's book is an important contribution to the history of TNR and in describing its effectiveness.

From humble beginnings in an alleyway in the nation's capital, Alley Cat Allies is now America's leading cat advocacy organization.

Above: *TNR Past, Present and Future: A History of the Trap-Neuter-Return Movement* by Ellen Perry Berkeley.

First Paws Forward

Launching TNR in 1990 was a tremendous challenge. The hurdles were steep and mistakes were made. Clearly, guidelines and written protocols were needed. Our first experience could be a model for others. We wrote factsheets when the people who found us out of their own determination (we did not have a dedicated phone or office yet) wanted to learn from us. The news of our efforts in the Adams Morgan alley with a group of cats quickly spread through the cat-loving community. We had already made dozens of calls to veterinary clinics, but only one would allow us to bring trapped feral cats in for treatment, and charged $500 for a spay surgery. We did not want others to reinvent the wheel. We were trained grassroots organizers who had the skills to create educational materials and mobilize advocates. What we did not know was the enormous number of people in the U.S. who would soon find us and help launch a national organization.
— Becky Robinson

ACHIEVEMENT 2

Feral Cats Need Allies

Making Connections with Our Feral Friends Network

Toby Franks wearing ACA's "I heart Feral Cats" T-shirt on the cover of the Tomahawk Live Trap Product Catalog, which is now a famous snapshot.

Quite soon after ACA began, we heard from increasing numbers of caregivers from across the country. They spoke about how they worked alone, felt isolated, and were fearful that the cats in the colony they looked after would be at risk if animal control found out about them. Some people wanted to know how they could help outdoor cats; others needed veterinary care for their colony. Still more worked to change policies or persuade decision makers.

We knew we couldn't be everywhere all the time to provide assistance to everyone who asked us for it. But we did realize that when we can't be there, others can. We had to figure out how we could put these compassionate Americans in touch with each other. So in our second year we established the Feral Friends Network. The FFN started as a list on paper, and we gave names out over the phone. Today we have a state-of-the-art system whereby the national, and increasingly international, network can be accessed on our website 24/7.

The FFN includes thousands of experienced trappers, colony caregivers, veterinarians, and spay/ neuter clinics across the country, who are actively protecting and improving the lives of cats. Every year we hear from thousands of people looking for help with cats.

For example, Nanelle Stine, who had been an FFN

Every year we hear from thousands of people looking for help with cats.

member for two years, received a request via FFN to help a lady learn how to TNR a female cat and her kittens whom she and a neighbor cared for jointly. They were both willing to share the surgery and vaccination fees. Nanelle helped them set up a shelter for the cats in one of their backyards. In addition to continuing to care for the cats with her neighbor, she subsequently volunteered as a backup feeder for a local feral cat colony, and became an active advocate for TNR and community cats in her county.

ACA worked with an FFN member organization,

People for Animals, and PFA's volunteer, Linda Nebesni. When a truck driver looking after nine cat colonies at a truck stop in Northern New Jersey needed help, ACA helped Linda and the caregiver carry out TNR, and 105 cats were spayed or neutered and vaccinated before being returned to their colonies. Funds were also raised to help with the veterinary costs.

On these occasions and many others like them, the FFN provides the support needed by sharing common experiences and discovering what others did in similar situations. Through their own efforts, they help to build a powerful network of caregivers and advocates. It was our responsibility to enable them with the means to do it. We needed to make the connection between the people looking for help and those who had experience in their community. Hence the FFN!

When someone becomes an FFN member, he or she:
- receives an Alley Cat Allies' Welcome Kit
- has access to ACA staff and materials
- has access to our members-only online listserv to connect with like-minded individuals and groups
- gains new volunteers and supporters and extends their services
- increases awareness by being a community resource

Without the FFN, the connection between ACA and Linda and Nanelle would have never been established. Every FFN member brings a list of contacts and resources that only expands the possibilities for helping cats.

Feral cats need friends, and felines have no better friend than Alley Cat Allies.

Challenging the Killing
Traveling America Teaching TNR

As Alley Cat Allies organizes and steps up efforts to teach America about Trap-Neuter-Return, the founders travel constantly, challenging the status quo by attending conferences, presenting workshops, distributing materials, and generally championing TNR for feral cats. Although we were initially met with resistance from established animal control and animal protection groups, and occasionally shunned from conferences for our "radical" ideas, the backlash backfired and attracted further attention to our cause.

The New Jersey Statewide Animal Rights Conference in 1991 was the first conference where we presented the ideas and practice of TNR. Only a few months after Alley Cat Allies was launched, this conference turned out to be a watershed for cats. We screened "The Control of Feral Cats," a 10-minute film produced by the Universities Federation for Animal Welfare in the U.K., which showed TNR's effectiveness.

The feedback we received afterwards at our table in the exhibit hall showed us that many attendees understood TNR to be the answer they needed to stop reproduction at their cat colonies. We could feel the energy from those who practically grabbed our handouts and sought one-on-one advice. People were hungry for information. They took away our brand new factsheets and copies of Ellen Perry Berkeley's book, *Maverick Cats*. Our Feral Friends Network was born through conversations at the conference and our collaboration with several ambitious New Jersey activists.

Slowly but surely we began to see the birth of this new cat protection movement and the need for Alley Cat Allies to become a national organization and the innovator in TNR for the U.S.

In 1994, all that changed when Esther Mechler, SPAY/USA's director and an early TNR supporter, included feral cats and TNR in the two-day conference program in Louisville, Kentucky.

TNR further became the issue to be debated and discussed at meetings everywhere. Our information and expertise were in demand. We became regular presenters at the SPAY/USA conferences for the following years. We were also invited to speak at national conferences, statewide humane society conferences, local shelter seminars, and eventually at animal control annual trainings. We crisscrossed the country from Los Angeles to Boston, Cheyenne, Wyoming to Miami.

Our mission was to tell the story of cats who aren't owned and don't need to be "rescued" and taken to shelters

> *We crisscrossed the country from Los Angeles to Boston, Cheyenne, Wyoming to Miami.*

where they would be killed. For too long in America we believed all cats need to be indoors, and if adoption wasn't an option, killing them was the kindest thing to do. We confronted this dogma head on. We made the logical case for TNR, with information from British experts, and our own experiences in Washington, D.C. We showed our photos of beautiful, healthy feral cats in alleyways as evidence of TNR's effectiveness. We shared the results of our efforts to spay and neuter 54 alley cats and place their kittens in homes. The colony was stable and there were no more litters of kittens being born, thanks to TNR.

Two points resonated with the audiences we spoke to that helped ignite the TNR revolution.

First, the vacuum effect was a new concept for many. You saw people nod their heads when they heard how new cats move in to take the place of any removed because of the available food, water, and shelter. The second key point was that cats can live outside, and the kindest act — as they're not candidates for adoption — is to not take them to the shelter. Cat lovers, and people who contacted us for help, embraced our appeal that cats don't need to go to the shelter. In fact, many of them had created their own ad hoc network of friends and family to take in the kittens.

We would hear about new TNR initiatives and veterinarians who learned new protocols, including how they spay and neuter feral cats who cannot be handled without being under anaesthesia. We are still in contact with those we met in 1991 at the first conference. We participate in as many conferences and local gatherings as we can to show how TNR is the way forward.

Coming Together for Cats

National Seminars Grow a Movement for Cat Protection

Alley Cat Allies is a proud organizer of meetings on TNR. Our seminar, Focus on Ferals — the first feral cat conference held in America — took place in Washington, D.C., in 1994. We brought together caregivers and experts from across the U.K., U.S., and Canada. Two of the world's leading international scientific authorities on feral cats, wildlife biologist Roger Tabor and veterinarian Dr. Jenny Remfry, came from the U.K. to address the audience about the biology of cats and the benefits of TNR.

Tabor focused on the cat in relation to the varied ecosystems in which the domestic cat is found. Drawing on his studies of cats worldwide as an author and television broadcaster, Tabor conveyed the importance of understanding the animal's biological makeup when dealing with population control. His presentation elaborated on feline home ranges in relation to breeding and looked at how those ranges are influenced by the availability of food.

Remfry described her work with feral cat colonies in Greece, Tunisia, Morocco, and the U.K. She described how to implement a TNR program and discussed its positive

Spokescat "Orwell T. Catt" and comic strip "Farley" by Phil Frank and comic strip farleycomicstrip.com. Credit: © Phil Frank.

We brought together caregivers and experts from across the U.K., U.S., and Canada.

results, including improvements in health and the significant reduction in fighting between males.

Tabor and Remfry were joined by Joanne Bruno of Animal Umbrella and AnnaBell Washburn of Pet Adoption and Welfare Services, Inc., to form a panel that answered questions from the attendees.

The politics of feral cat colony management programs were addressed by Dan Knapp of the Sonoma County Humane Society in California and by Laura Nelson of the George Mason University School of Law, including "How to Fight City Hall." They provided practical guidance for building positive relationships with key officials and for promoting favorable government ordinances.

Additional speakers included Dr. Andrew Rowan of the Tufts University Center for Animals and Public Policy and Gloria Parkinson, editor of the newsletter *Catnip*.

Focus on Ferals was followed by more conferences between 1994 and 2005 and in 2013 when we held our next meeting. Becky Robinson spoke at many other meetings and seminars organized by national and local animal rights organizations and local shelters and SPCAs.

Speaking out for cats will always be a mission that ACA gladly undertakes.

Trap-Neuter-Return Ordinances

The Future of Animal Control

The first local Trap-Neuter-Return ordinances were passed and major city shelters began practicing TNR in the mid-1990s.

Our research in 2013 and 2014 showed that at least 500 local governments have enacted ordinances or policies supporting TNR. (See "Trap-Neuter-Return Ordinances and Policies in the United States: The Future of Animal Control" by Elizabeth Holtz, JD at www.alleycat.org.)

In the United States today, at least 523 cities and counties officially support or recognize TNR. The three states with the highest number of TNR ordinances are New Jersey (65), Texas (42), and California (37). Major municipalities and counties that support TNR include San Francisco, the District of Columbia, New York City, Sacramento County and San Jose (California), Palm Beach County (Florida), Clark County (Nevada), Philadelphia, Pittsburgh, Las Vegas, Broward County (Florida), Cook County (Illinois), Oklahoma City, Dallas, Omaha, St. Paul, Milwaukee, Salt Lake City, Fairfax County (Virginia), and Suffolk County (New York).

TNR is endorsed by local governments ranging from conservative Colorado Springs, Colorado, to liberal Berkeley, California. Because TNR decreases the size of colonies, reduces animal control calls from citizens, improves public health, and is humane and economical, it is an appealing method of community cat care for many different interest groups and organizations, not all of them related to animal protection. This has resulted in an extraordinary diversity of communities with TNR that vary in population, region of the country, and political orientation.

Our research shows, however, it is not always necessary or even advantageous to pursue an ordinance if the local codes present no obstacle for the neutering and returning of unowned cats.

This approach may seem counterintuitive because animal advocates usually regard laws that protect animals as positive. Even well-intentioned laws can end up causing more harm than good if they create

regulations and restrictions — and subsequently, penalties and liabilities — where there were none. For example, detailed and unnecessary regulations regarding the care of feral cats could result in caregivers being fined if they fail to follow them exactly. Also, cats could be impounded and killed — even if they already have been neutered and vaccinated — if they are not part of what could be deemed "sanctioned" or "registered" colonies.

Often, our recommendation is that brief ordinances that simply communicate the city's support are best. For example, the Washington, D.C., ordinance underscores the city's commitment to TNR without regulating the practice of TNR. It states that the animal control agency "shall promote: (1) the reduction of euthanasia of animals for which medical treatment or adoption is possible; and (2) the utilization of trap, spay or neuter, and return practices as a means of controlling the feral cat population."

TNR is endorsed by local governments ranging from conservative Colorado Springs, Colorado, to liberal Berkeley, California.

Finally, it is important to note that an ordinance, or the lack thereof, may not provide a clear picture of actual TNR practices in a community. A municipality may have an admirable TNR ordinance, but without education and support from animal control services and community members, the cats are unlikely to benefit. Conversely, there may be a thriving TNR program but no TNR ordinance.

The primary goal is for TNR to be a regular and accepted practice in communities. An ordinance is one tool among many to achieve this objective. There are guidelines to follow to ensure any ordinance passed best protects cats and caregivers.

The research is clear: TNR is the future of animal control and sheltering. TNR is embraced by hundreds of local governments in the U.S., and is becoming the primary method of community cat management.

Hotline for Cats!

National Cat Help Desk Answers the Calls

Doris and Nichol started at opposite sides of the spectrum: Doris wanted to trap and remove cats living at the mobile home park in Florida where she was a manager, while Nichol, a resident and college student, wanted the cats to remain.

Enter ACA's National Cat Help Desk. After hearing from one of Nichol's family members, a specialist from our newly launched team started communicating with both parties. She effectively promoted the benefits of TNR to Doris and convinced her that it was the best approach for the whole community, and then encouraged Nichol to start learning the ropes and implement TNR.

From what seemed like a discouraging start, this situation became another success story for the community and the cats. What our staff specialist found was not unique. With the right tools and the full story — that community cats live their lives content in their outdoor colony, but face certain death if brought to shelters — individuals with different opinions about cats often find common ground.

Although we had a help desk from day one, we didn't call it that until we launched the National Cat Help Desk in 2012. Our first year and very first "achievement" was carrying out TNR in the Adams Morgan alley in Washington, D.C. The reason we formed ACA was so that we could help others with step-by-step factsheets and advice. We didn't want people to have to reinvent the wheel. We knew there was a need when hundreds of people found us before we ever had an office or business phone line. Our home phones rang and our answering machines were full every day before we came up with our organization's name, Alley Cat Allies. We responded to 600 requests via email and phone in the first official month after our help desk launch in 2012 from all parts of the country and a few from people in other countries. Now, every year, we respond to thousands of requests for help with cats from individuals, organizations, and businesses. The number steadily increases each month.

The National Cat Help Desk is the first of its kind. Our team provides one-on-one assistance and a caring,

Now, every year, we respond to thousands of requests for help with cats from individuals, organizations, and businesses.

supportive ear for people all across the country. The requests cover all aspects of our work. There are the calls and emails that involve the straightforward sharing of resources: connecting people to our Feral Friends Network, talking people through the steps of TNR, and sharing links to our online educational resources. Then there are the inquiries where we must become more involved, such as the one in Florida. In these cases, we draw on our 25 years of mediation and problem-solving experience to help others stop local threats to cats, or organize grassroots efforts to help cats.

Connect with the National Cat Help Desk online at www.alleycat.org/GetHelp or via phone at (240) 482-1980, ext. 330.

Top 10 Publications Available from Alley Cat Allies

1. How to Live with Cats in Your Neighborhood
2. "We're Helping Outdoor Cats" (door hanger)
3. Discover the Truth About Feral Cats
4. Community Cat Infographic poster
5. Feral and Stray Cats – An Important Difference
6. Feral Cats and the Public: A Healthy Relationship
7. "Don't Call Animal Control" (door hanger)
8. Rabies: A Public Health Victory
9. Biology and Behavior of the Cat
10. Public Opinion on Humane Treatment of Stray Cats

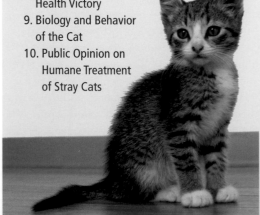

Discover the Truth About Community Cats

Community cats have existed alongside people for 10,000 years.
They are not a new phenomenon. Community cats, also called feral or outdoor cats, live and thrive in every landscape, from the inner city to rural farmland.

Most community cats are not socialized to people.
And therefore, they are not adoptable. They don't belong indoors and are typically wary of us. However, as members of the domestic cat species (just like pet cats), they are protected under state anti-cruelty laws.

Community cats should not be taken to pounds and shelters.
Community cats' needs are not met by animal control agencies or shelters. They live full, healthy lives outdoors—but are usually killed in shelters. Even no-kill shelters can't place unsocialized cats in homes.

Their kittens can be adopted.
Kittens can often be adopted into homes, but they must be socialized at an early age. There is a crucial window, and if they aren't handled in time, they will remain feral and therefore unadoptable.

alleycat.org

Alley Cat Allies
©2015
7920 Norfolk Avenue, Suite 600
Bethesda, MD 20814
www.alleycat.org

We're Helping Outdoor Cats

Here Are a Few Ways You Can Help, Too

LOCAL ORGANIZATION CONTACT

will humanely trap, neuter, and return community cats in your neighborhood on

Trap-Neuter-Return benefits the cats and the neighborhood. All of the community cats—also called feral cats—are going to be spayed or neutered, vaccinated, and eartipped the universal symbol of a neutered and vaccinated cat. Back in their outdoor home, they will not reproduce—no more kittens! Trap-Neuter-Return improves their lives and yours. It is effective and humane—other approaches for community cats just don't work.

- **Keep your** ... accidental...
- **Contact** ... or surrou... eat and...
- **Don't t** ... (always) ... traps ... inside ... our t...

Alley Cat Allies
25 Years of Advocacy

How to Live With Cats in Your Neighborhood

COMMUNITY CAT

ALSO KNOWN AS: Outdoor Cat, Stray Cat, Alley Cat, Feral Cat, Street Cat, Barn Cat, and Tomcat.

Outdoor community cats and pet cats are the same species—*Felis catus*—the domestic cat.

An eartip is the universal symbol to identify a neutered and vaccinated cat. The top ⅜ inch of the cat's left ear is removed during surgery.

Community cats are **not adoptable** because they are not socialized to humans.

Studies show outdoor cats are as **healthy** as pet cats and can have the same life span.

"Feral" describes behavior—feral cats are wary of people and live on their own outdoors.

More than 40% of Americans have cared for an outdoor cat.

Cats live everywhere.	Outdoor cats live in family groups called **colonies**.	**More than 70%** of all cats who go to a shelter are killed there.	**Removing community cats doesn't work.** Catching and killing is ineffective, outdated, and cruel.	**Trap-Neuter-Return (TNR)** is the only humane, effective approach to care for community cats. Cats are **spayed or neutered**, **vaccinated**, and eartipped and then returned to their outdoor home.
Cats have lived outdoors alongside humans since **before the pyramids**.	Cats are **bonded** to their environments and colonies.	For community cats, that rises to **virtually 100%**.		

 Alley Cat Allies   Learn more about community cats at alleycat.org/GetInformed.

Community Cat Health Care

Our First Free Monthly Spay/Neuter Clinic

ACA launched and financed the monthly Northern Virginia No-Cost Feral Cat Spay/Neuter Clinic in 1998. Our clinic was the first and only free spay/neuter service for feral cats in the Washington, D.C., metropolitan area. As word quickly spread about the clinic, people and their cats came from seven states, including West Virginia.

On our first day, two *pro bono* veterinarians and three volunteers sterilized and vaccinated 10 feral cats. Soon clinic veterinarians were sterilizing and treating as many as 100 cats in one day. Over the next 10 years, we were responsible for spaying or neutering and vaccinating more than 6,500 cats. The clinic usually had a crew of 40 volunteers on Sundays.

Dr. Alison Mocko led the clinic's volunteer veterinarians since its inception. Her team had great success with their implementation of juvenile spay/neuter. By practicing early-age sterilization — kittens who are at least two months old or weigh more than two pounds — the clinic's veterinarians ensured that hundreds of cats did not slip through the cracks and begin reproducing simply because of their young age at the time of trapping. Dr. Jamie Netschert generously shared his spacious, state-of-the-art animal hospital and volunteered by performing hundreds of surgeries.

First envisioned by Becky Robinson as a way to address a critical need in the area, our clinic expanded over the years as community cat advocacy evolved.

The Northern Virginia No-Cost Feral Cat Spay/Neuter Clinic was the catalyst for many exciting developments for community cats in the region. For example, we persuaded Fairfax County to host our TNR workshop and give TNR information to citizens who called about cats. We also encouraged them to establish a TNR shelter program. We made a video with Fairfax County in which they recognized they had changed their policy and made a paradigm shift in the animal control and shelter system by implementing a full-fledged TNR program

Further, Fairfax County showed how it was possible to secure support and commitment from local communities, and it's now one of the nation's leaders in championing TNR. It all started when we offered spay/neuter and vaccination services to volunteers who

Over the next 10 years, we were responsible for spaying or neutering and vaccinating more than 6,500 cats.

trapped cats and brought them to our Sunday clinic. We demonstrated the need for a clinic that operated throughout the month and not simply one day a month. The clinic was made possible with thanks to such volunteers and grassroots groups as Lori Anglin and Metro Ferals, Pam Draper and Dewey Animals, Inc., Barbara Becker and The Humane Society of Fairfax County, and Teresa Kappes and Cat's Cradle.

The Northern Virginia No-Cost Feral Cat Spay/Neuter Clinic was a significant achievement because it was the first of its kind. It was managed by an amazing group of volunteers and veterinarians who donated their services. It was precedent-setting and cutting-edge, attracting many visitors who then went on to establish similar clinics and TNR programs in their area.

Roll Call

Many volunteers, caregivers, grassroots groups, and veterinarians generously and repeatedly volunteered their time and expertise to make possible the Northern Virginia No-Cost Feral Cat Spay/Neuter Clinic.

For example, the following veterinarians provided invaluable spay/neutering service: Dr. Hope Baird, Dr. Nicole Chevalier, Dr. Jana Froeling, Dr. Marisa Gerth, Dr. Sandra Marshall, Dr. Lisa Osier, Dr. Jan Rosen, Dr. Robin Valentine, Dr. Elton Vyfhuis, and Dr. Alison Mocko, Head Veterinarian and many others.

ACHIEVEMENT 8

Cats Under the Boardwalk
Atlantic City Stops Killing and Adopts TNR

No one knows when the feral cats first appeared under New Jersey's Atlantic City boardwalk. For years, they coexisted with residents, mingled with tourists, and were generally tolerated by city officials. So when animal control began trapping and killing the boardwalk cats in 2000, ACA stepped in to save them and their longstanding relationship with the city and its visitors.

Shortly after learning of the trapping that first took a mother cat and left her newborn kittens behind, we formed the Cat Action Team with Atlantic City's Health Department, the Humane Society of Atlantic County (HSAC), and local caregivers and advocates. Under ACA's leadership, the group began a highly successful pilot program using Trap-Neuter-Return, community involvement, and public education to save the lives of the 350 cats then calling the boardwalk home.

In June 2000, ACA staff began trapping and transporting cats to HSAC on a monthly basis to be neutered. A third of the cats trapped were young kittens or cats socialized enough to be placed up for adoption. The rest were returned to the boardwalk sporting "eartips" indicating they were neutered and vaccinated. As TNR took effect, births of new kittens at the boardwalk gradually ceased, and the population has naturally and humanely declined by 72 percent in 15 years.

Now formally known as the Boardwalk Cats Project (BCP), it receives outspoken support from Atlantic City's local government, as well as many local businesses along the boardwalk. The public also responds positively through donations of cash and cat food.

Since we interceded on their behalf, the boardwalk cats' lives have improved dramatically. Every colony has been completely neutered. Spared from being killed, they were also relieved of the toll breeding can take on a cat's health.

BCP is still going strong. The boardwalk is home to neutered cats living in stable colonies and monitored

> *Since we interceded on their behalf, the boardwalk cats' lives have improved dramatically.*

by devoted volunteer caregivers.

Shelters and feeding stations keep the cats warm and dry. As an added bonus for the community, volunteers help beautify the boardwalk by regularly hosting clean-ups. To support caregivers, ACA devotes two on-site staff coordinators to BCP and other local programs. Signs posted along the boardwalk discourage feeding the cats by anyone other than project-coordinated volunteer caregivers. They also explain the laws and penalties around abandoning cats at the site, and give contact information for volunteering with Alley Cat Allies.

In 2008, Atlantic City joined ACA's Every Kitty — Every City program, which rallies support, raises awareness, and provides resources for implementing

Becky Robinson with Atlantic City Department of Health and Human Services director Ron Cash celebrating the success of the Boardwalk Cats Project.

This outreach poster helps brings awareness about our Boardwalk Cats Project.

Alf is a feral cat... who lives in a colony near the boardwalk. Alley Cat Allies cares for the cats as part of a city supported Trap-Neuter-Return program. Learn more at: www.alleycat.org/AtlanticCity.

Boardwalk Cats Project.
You can help. Alley Cat Allies

WWW.ALLEYCAT.ORG

TNR and accessible, affordable spay and neuter services for all cats citywide.

BCP is a model program for the nation and shows that TNR works. The cats, many of whom are now in their teens, are living proof that cats live long and healthy lives outdoors. These famous cats draw visitors and admirers from all over the country.

Thanks to ACA, the cats living under Atlantic City's famous boardwalk coexist harmoniously with the city's people and visitors. No municipality need ever turn to killing cats.

The cats at the Boardwalk are helped throughout the year by compassionate volunteers.

A C H I E V E M E N T 9

U.S. Military Makes It Official

TNR Makes Rank at U.S. Naval Shipyard

Becky Robinson of ACA, NNSY feral cat caretaker Cynthia Moose, Kim Isaacs of ACA, and Michael Brayshaw of NNSY stand behind the thousands of postcards sent to NNSY commander, Captain Mark Hugel, supporting the shipyard's feral cats.
Credit: Steve Milner.

Alley Cat Allies became the first animal group in the world, as far as we are aware, to hold a TNR contract with the U.S. military.

In 2000, ACA learned that officials at the Norfolk Naval Shipyard (NNSY) in Portsmouth, Virginia, had banned a local longtime employee from her regular efforts of feeding and providing veterinary care for cats living at the shipyard. Officials planned to contract within weeks for the U.S. Department of Agriculture's Wildlife Services to trap and kill the cats at a cost of more than $21,000 taxpayer dollars. To make matters worse, the trapping was planned during a period in which there was a serious risk of separating lactating mothers from their young kittens.

We quickly took action, contacting shipyard officials and offering educational information about the benefits of colony care, including neutering and vaccination for the cats, and pressing for the caregiver's access to the cats to be reinstated. We explained that "catch and kill" was not only cruel but also expensive and ineffective. We noted that some U.S. municipalities had begun embracing TNR as a cost-effective and humane program for feral cats.

After initial requests to meet with shipyard officials were ignored, ACA launched a publicity campaign aimed at mobilizing the public and pressing the shipyard

to end the "catch and kill" plan and meet with us. We spearheaded a letter-writing effort in which thousands of supporters wrote to the shipyard's leadership protesting the plan. We also organized a public demonstration outside the shipyard gates that garnered the attention of the local media.

The shipyard leadership remained skeptical, but the publicity surrounding the campaign persuaded them to sit at the table with us. After days of negotiations, the shipyard representatives agreed to a formal contract with us to carry out a nonlethal, humane plan for the shipyard colonies, saying they would "defer to [Alley Cat Allies] as the experts." Alley Cat Allies became the first animal group in the world, as far as we are aware, to hold a TNR contract with the U.S. military.

Under the contract, ACA organized a comprehensive program alongside local feral cat experts, including members of Meower Power, some of whom had clearance to enter the shipyard. Volunteers carried out trapping and ongoing colony management, as well as constructed permanent feeding stations in designated areas and provided veterinary services to neuter and vaccinate the cats.

In recognition of the fact that TNR has stabilized the population and allowed the cats to coexist peacefully alongside shipyard operations, the Norfolk Naval Shipyard reported that the program was highly effective. The military is top-down and highly bureaucratic, and while there was strong support for humane programs for the shipyard cats, a technical memorandum curtailed the formal TNR program and contract. However, the cats who were returned to their colonies are neutered, vaccinated, and eartipped, and the employees are fond of them.

Cats on Campus
TNR Gets Good Grades

Amid the students, professors, and administrators, there are other residents on college campuses: cats. You may not even notice them at first. They typically hide during the day and come out at night, and they are generally leery of humans.

ACA launched the Cats on Campus program after hearing from students, employees, and faculty across the country. The program recognizes the unique hurdles and needs of caring for cat colonies at educational institutions. We wrote materials and formed an online CampusCats listserv, a place for groups to network and connect, share experiences and knowledge, and provide support.

TNR improves the lives of cats, as they are healthier and do not experience the strains of mating or pregnancy.

With proper resources and information, caring individuals can learn how to trap cats for neutering. TNR improves the lives of cats, as they are healthier and do not experience the strains of mating or pregnancy.

Uninformed administrators may attempt to trap and remove the cats. However well intended, this approach ends with cats being impounded at the local shelter where they are killed at taxpayer expense. Removing cats from an area creates a vacuum, which more cats will move into and breed to fill.

Scientific studies prove TNR works on college campuses and improves cats' relationship with the campus community. For example, a long-term study on the University of Central Florida campus found that TNR keeps cat colonies stable and healthy. The 11-year study, by Dr. Julie Levy and Leslie and David Gale, observed that the number of cats on campus declined by 66 percent, with no new kittens born after the first four years of operation. At the end of the study, most of the remaining cats were older: 83 percent had been part of the program for more than six years, indicating a healthy lifespan for feral cats after TNR.

TNR makes the grade!

TNR on Campus

TNR programs have been successfully implemented on campuses across the nation for the past two decades, including:

Stanford University — Stanford Cat Network

Texas A&M University College Station — Aggie Feral Cat Alliance of Texas

University of California at Davis — The Feline Medicine Club: Orphan Kitten Project

The University of Texas at Austin — The Campus Cats Coalition

Towson University — Tiny Tigers

Arizona State University — Mild Cats

Seven Easy Steps

1. Gather information
2. Organize volunteers; include students, employees, and faculty
3. Contact your school's administration
4. Coordinate a campus TNR plan
5. Work with local veterinarians
6. Organize colony care; identify a local professor or employee with long-term commitment to cats as the program leader
7. Set up an adoption program for socialized cats and kittens

Stanford Cat Network

The Stanford Alumni Magazine's November/December 1998 issue recognized the achievements of the Stanford Cat Network, a group of faculty, students and staff who cared for the 150 cats on the campus. The magazine reports founding member Carole Hyde, a project associate at the Institute for International Studies, as saying volunteers registered 500 cats in 1989 and the cat population was down by 70 percent in 1998. The program spays, neuters and, when possible, finds homes for the cats. Universities from Texas to Virginia have started programs modeled on Stanford's.

ACHIEVEMENT 11

National Feral Cat Day

A Call to Action for Saving Cats

National Feral Cat Day (NFCD) is the biggest day of the year for cats.

Alley Cat Allies launched National Feral Cat Day on our 10th anniversary in 2001. We created National Feral Cat Day and selected October 16 because it's the date of our incorporation (October 16, 1991). Our mission for this annual campaign is to raise awareness about domestic cats (including outdoor cats), promote TNR, and mobilize the millions of compassionate Americans who care for these cats. In 2013 we timed our conference, "Architects of Change for Cats: Building blueprints for humane communities," so that it would be part of that year's National Feral Cat Day national outreach.

Every year, National Feral Cat Day has a theme and a colorful poster that rallies cat lovers and advocates everywhere to participate.

Every year, National Feral Cat Day has a theme and a colorful poster that rallies cat lovers and advocates everywhere to participate. The campaign has materials specifically designed for our advocacy kit, including booklets about Organizing and Promoting Events, Organizing a Spay Day for Feral Cats, and Holding a Fundraiser Walk-a-Thon, plus instructions for conducting a cat food drive, and more recently, a Social Media Toolkit in addition to our existing Media Guide. And, of course, each year a T-shirt design with the theme is sent to event organizers with their NFCD toolkit. In 2015, the kit has a kitten nursing bottle for saving orphaned kittens, as well as tips for properly disinfecting traps and cages. The Tru-Catch and Tomahawk trap companies and the ACES (Animal Care Equipment and Services) company offer special discounts for National Feral Cat Day.

The first official National Feral Cat Day poster was created by Phil Frank in 2001.

National Feral Cat Day and National Media

Awareness about National Feral Cat Day has increasingly made its way into popular media. In 2009, the answer to a "Jeopardy" game show question – "National ____ Cat Day" – was "Feral." On Conan O'Brien's talk show, Andy Richter gave a humorous account of his participation with NCFD in 2011. Actress Edie Falco and cat behaviorist/TV show host Jackson Galaxy recorded public service announcements urging the public to help support community cats.

National Feral Cat Day has events in all 50 states now. Public awareness has been raised as a result of the hundreds of news stories every October about local NFCD events. Pennsylvania, Reno, NV, and many others ratified resolutions that embrace TNR. NFCD has sparked new organizations to form, and has been the catalyst for the humane movement to unite and grow which is why TNR is mainstream today.

This is why the theme of our 2015 event is "The Evolution of the Cat Revolution." More and more people join National Feral Cat Day each year. In 2012, 450 events were held nationally, with some held internationally. The year before that, there were 351 events, which was almost twice as many as in 2010.

National Feral Cat Day continues to grow every year and advance cat advocacy!

Join us and learn more at the National Feral Cat Day website www.nationalferalcatday.org.

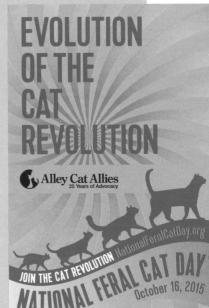

Feral Cats Take the Stand

Our Lawsuit Saves Lives

In 2003 Alley Cat Allies sued the Florida Fish and Wildlife Conservation Commission (FWC) because it had adopted a policy ("Impacts of Domestic Cats on Native Wildlife") that banned TNR and encouraged cats to be killed.

Our petition, which was also brought by Dr. Frank Hamilton, a resident of Hillsborough County, Florida, argued that the FWC's policy would not only ban TNR programs already successfully operating in the state, but would also reach onto private lands and regulate cats on private property. We also argued that materials used by FWC policymakers to assess the impact of feral cats on

This was an important lawsuit involving ACA because it meant that thousands of cats' lives were saved, and caregivers in Florida could continue to care for feral cats unhindered.

native wildlife were not based on sound science.

Although Administrative Law Judge David M. Maloney dismissed our case, he ruled that the FWC policy was not a formal law and could not be enforced.

This was an important lawsuit involving ACA because it meant that thousands of cats' lives were saved, and caregivers in Florida could continue to care for feral cats unhindered.

Florida agencies must follow specific public procedures when issuing rules that have the force of law — procedures the FWC admitted were not followed. In his ruling, the judge made it clear that unless and until the agency formally adopts a rule to manage feral cat populations, the policy adopted by FWC regarding feral cats is simply a policy and not a law it could enforce.

Becky Robinson said the ruling meant that "Communities across Florida currently using TNR as an effective means to reduce feral cat colonies can legally continue to do so, and new TNR programs can be implemented. Should the FWC decide to issue an actual rule with the power of law, it will have to follow the

public rule-making procedures. At that point, ACA, TNR experts and cat lovers from all across Florida will introduce the peer-reviewed scientific studies alluded to by Judge Maloney, as well as other solid evidence that proves TNR is in fact the only effective method to stabilize feral cat populations."

Alley Cat Allies compiled an important advocacy tool for citizens in Florida, "Protect Florida's Cats Campaign Media Handbook," during the campaign before the FWC ruled on its policy.

TNR programs are flourishing in Florida, including ones in Jacksonville (Feral Freedom), Hillsborough County, Manatee County, Lake County, Miami/Dade County Animal Services, Lee County, and Alachua County. The Florida Animal Friend License Plate program has awarded grants to several TNR organizations for spay, neuter, and vaccination of cats.

FWC Policy Revised

After the judge's decision, there was a roundtable meeting held by the FWC commissioner that ACA attended. FWC revised their policy on outdoor cats and TNR because of our lawsuit. They stated:

- The FWC will NOT initiate a campaign to eradicate outdoor cats
- After reviewing comments received on our draft policy, the FWC modified the policy to remove reference to trap-neuter-return programs as an ineffective technique to reduce feral cat numbers

Turning Tragedy into Triumph

Learning from Hurricane Katrina

Ten years later, Hurricane Katrina remains ranked as the third most intense storm of its kind to make landfall in the U.S. More than 1,800 people died in the 2005 hurricane and subsequent flooding. Property damage was estimated to be at least $108 billion. Of course,

Our phones began to ring because residents who left their cats behind were not allowed to return home to save them.

many animals suffered and died, too. An estimated 600,000 pets were killed or left without shelter as a result of Hurricane Katrina. The exact number will never be known.

ACA is not a disaster response organization. But it quickly became apparent that for every forlorn dog caught on camera in New Orleans and the surrounding area impacted by the hurricane, a frightened, hungry cat was hiding, unseen by those who could help.

Homes were flooded and people were in their attics and on their roofs. When helicopters and boats were saving people, their animals were turned away. Since animals are members of the family, we were not surprised to learn that people in New Orleans refused to evacuate without their companion animals. Those who were evacuated from the Superdome were not allowed to take their pets with them.

Our phones began to ring because residents who left their cats behind were not allowed to return home to save them. ACA had to act. We organized equipment, supplies, and volunteers. Our team at headquarters searched for suitable locations for a base camp near New Orleans. A plea for assistance was issued on our social media.

In a matter of hours, ACA supporter Emily Canter put us in contact with her mother, Millicent Canter, who offered us the use of her property outside Bogalusa as an emergency shelter and volunteer base camp. Bogalusa is about 80 miles

north of New Orleans. ACA's Bonney Brown lead our response effort, and the first of our hearty volunteers made their way into the hurricane zone.

Over the next three months, 361 stray, feral, and pet cats rescued from ravaged areas, along with 150 volunteers (including veterinarians and veterinary technicians) from across the nation, passed through the Bogalusa camp. Hundreds of other cats in Louisiana and Mississippi received food, veterinary care, and a chance to live, thanks to the outpouring of support from donors old and new.

Hurricane Katrina shed a sobering light on the inadequate and inhumane animal evacuation and rescue protocol during natural disasters. In the days following Katrina, local shelters refused entry to cats taken there by evacuated pet owners. Residents of a mobile home community helped us save a colony of 77 feral cats, even as they were being evicted to make way for FEMA trailers. Hundreds of cats were left behind and forgotten in the flooded homes and streets of New Orleans – frightened, lost, and hungry.

Everywhere we went, there were cats in need and people struggling to care for them. We made it our mission to help them both. We knew that TNR was the best way to improve the lives of the thousands of intact

"Turning Devastation into Dedication: Outreach in New Orleans" declared our report in the *Alley Cat Action* newsletter.

Cries for Help

In the days after Hurricane Katrina made landfall, calls and emails poured into Alley Cat Allies:

"We had several cats living in the courtyard. They have been neutered and cared for by the cafe staff. They're probably still waiting there."

"Can someone rescue my cat...the balcony door can be jimmied open and there's a cat carrier. Please help save her!"

"There is a colony of cats that are living under the docks. Please get some food to them."

"Please help. We have two cats stranded in our house in New Orleans…They are our world..."

"There are many feral colonies near where the 17th Street levee breach occurred."

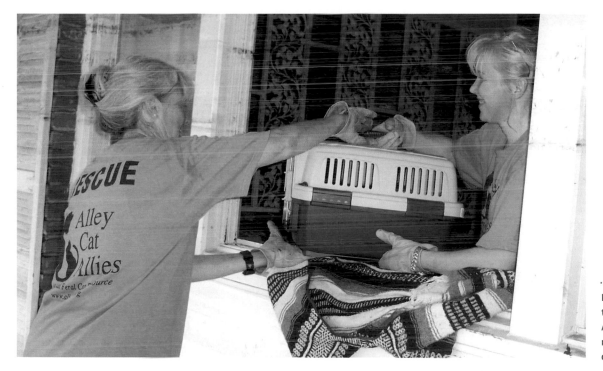

In the aftermath of the storm, Alley Cat Allies helping to rescue thousands of displaced cats.

cats now living on the streets of New Orleans. And so we organized the Feline Frenzy spay/neuter marathon in 2006 and spayed or neutered and vaccinated 1,166 cats free of charge for grateful residents. Then we organized the Feline Forum, a pair of workshops that empowered Gulf area residents and animal control workers to maintain their own TNR programs. We also donated humane box traps, cat carriers, and other supplies to aid in cat recovery and care to MomaKat Rescue in Birmingham, Alabama, and the Tuscaloosa Metro Animal Shelter.

As New Orleans gradually rebuilt in the years following Katrina, we stayed in touch and helped promote organizations and individuals caring for cats, just as we have since our work began there 20 years ago. Today, New Orleans is part of our Every Kitty – Every City program, which raises awareness about the importance and availability of affordable neuter services for all cats — pet, stray, and feral — and provides a place where caregivers, volunteers, and residents can network, find help for feral cats in their communities, and continue to come together for cats after Katrina.

In 2008, ACA received the Friendship Key to the City of New Orleans presented by the Humane Society of Louisiana for our work to save the city's cats. We were deeply honored, but our lasting reward has been seeing services for cats expand and life improve for the cats of New Orleans and the people who care about them.

In 2011, ACA announced a grant of $20,000 to the Louisiana SPCA and the Southern Animal Foundation to offer fully subsidized spay/neuter services for feral and stray cats in Greater New Orleans.

There's even more reason to celebrate!

New state and federal laws, including the Pet Evacuation and Transportation Standards (PETS) Act, specifically address the management of displaced animals within disaster planning protocols to mitigate such chaos and confusion when the next disaster strikes.

Enormous strides have taken place with regard to cat protection policies since Hurricane Katrina. For example, the Humane Society of Louisiana, Plaquemines Cat Action Team, and the Louisiana SPCA now regularly educate the general public about TNR.

ACA will stay focused on our mission to transform and develop communities to protect and improve the lives of cats until our job is done.

Hurricane Katrina Volunteer Roll Call

Many people helped in many ways after Hurricane Katrina, including a later rescue of 77 cats from Michael Court, a trailer park outside New Orleans that was condemned. All of their kindness is appreciated, including the 150 volunteers from across the nation who gave their time and expertise at the Bogalusa camp. Some of those who deserve special recognition include Diane Blankenburg, Bonney Brown, Dr. Marcus Brown, Millicent Canter, Dr. Karyen Chu, Jim Davis, Thelma Guarraggi, Laura Guimond, Rebecca Guinn, Dr. Kate Howard, Kim Kean, Julie Linford, Karen Little, Kerry Moyers-Horton, Valerie Schumacher, Dr. Richard Speck, and Karlyn Sturmer.

ACHIEVEMENT 14

Leading the Way

Nation's Capital Embraces Feral Cats and TNR

Right: **Alley Cat Allies creates the pilot TNR initiative, DC Cat Assistance Team – DC CAT, the program that was pivotal in changing policy to save cats in our nation's capital.**

Another development for TNR in the Washington, D.C., metropolitan area was our decision to become a founding financial supporter of the Washington Humane Society's (WHS) National Capital Area Spay and Neuter Center, which supports their CatNIPP program for feral cats.

Before 2004, area residents who sought assistance with stray and feral cats by calling animal control often found that their calls resulted in the cats being trapped and killed. (In Washington, animal control is contracted out to the privately run WHS and overseen by the D.C. Department of Public Health.)

As with the vast majority of outdoor cats across the country, the District's feral cats are healthy, but they are unadoptable because they are not socialized to people. The city's previous catch-and-kill policy led to

The city's previous catch-and-kill policy led to thousands of needless deaths in shelters each year, at considerable cost to taxpayers.

thousands of needless deaths in shelters each year, at considerable cost to taxpayers. In 2004, ACA approached the DPH with a proposal to establish a pilot TNR program. The goals were to demonstrate to

skeptical public health and animal control officials how TNR humanely and effectively stabilizes feral cat colonies, and to show that their existing policy was failing. The magnitude of animals being killed each year not only made up a sizeable portion of the millions of dollars spent on animal control and sheltering, but was needless and inhumane.

The DPH accepted the pilot program — which was funded primarily by ACA — and promoted it to city residents as a partnership between the department, ACA, and other local animal protection organizations, including the Washington Animal Rescue League and Metro Ferals.

Under the pilot program, called DC CAT (District of Columbia Cat Assistance Team), animal control officers and shelter officials referred calls about feral cats to ACA, which then worked with residents and volunteers to humanely trap the cats and bring them to local clinics for subsidized spay/neuter and other veterinary services. As established by ACA's best-practice standards for TNR, feral cats brought to the clinics had a small portion of the left ear removed (called an "eartip") to identify them as already neutered and vaccinated. Tame cats and young kittens found in neighborhoods entered foster care provided by volunteers until permanent homes were found.

DC CAT

DC CAT ASSISTANCE TEAM

ACA was also responsible for recruiting volunteers and training animal control officers and shelter workers on TNR and mediation techniques.

During the first year of the program, ACA fielded more than 250 calls from residents seeking help with outdoor cats, and more than 1,400 cats were neutered and vaccinated. In addition to training and coordinating volunteers, ACA organized community workshops on humane care for outdoor cats, and used door hangers and leaflets to teach residents about ways to humanely deter cats from gardens, cars, and the like.

Due in large part to the program's great success, WHS announced in 2006 that it would embrace TNR as an effective means of stabilizing the feral cat population in the city, and established a monthly subsidized spay/neuter clinic for feral cats. In 2007, WHS opened the city's first high-volume clinic, the National Capital Area Spay and Neuter Center, which included a permanent no-cost program for feral cats. ACA was a founding financial supporter of the center.

In 2008, the city passed a law that required the Animal Care and Control Agency to promote TNR practices to manage the feral cat population, provided that all efforts are made to adopt out trapped, tamable kittens.

We're proud of our relationship with the animal control and shelter agencies in Washington, D.C., and of the difference we've all made to the lives of cats living in the nation's capital. Under the leadership of Lisa Lafontaine and Scott Giacoppo, WHS is a model in the country and world for its humane programs for cats. WHS awarded Becky Robinson the "Humane Hero Award" in 2015 and said it was proud to be the shelter and animal control agency in the city where TNR began in the United States.

ACHIEVEMENT 15

Nothing "Necessary" About This Evil

The Beginning of a Much-Needed Paradigm Shift

From early on, Alley Cat Allies wanted to understand exactly where the threat to cats came from. The "problem" of outdoor cats in our community defied definition. Many assessments were made until we realized what was being seen as the "problem" was the exact opposite.

First, it was considered the public's fault. They didn't care about outdoor cats and wanted them removed from their neighborhoods. But we found from all of our hands-on and front-line work in the Washington, D.C., metropolitan area and Atlantic City, New Jersey, that this wasn't true. People from all backgrounds and ages came forward to help. They wanted the cats to live but not reproduce, and donated their time to our TNR programs.

Second, it was thought to be the cat caregivers' fault. They were issued citations from their municipalities and animal control for noncompliance with local laws because, it was decreed, when you care for outdoor cats you legally own them. But feral cats can't be "owned" by anyone and that's why we have "caregivers." Compassionate people weren't guilty of any crime.

Third, there wasn't enough money for large-scale TNR programs in entire communities. But we found people who opened their wallets as they did their hearts to support humane, nonlethal programs.

For these reasons, Alley Cat Allies insists that a new animal control system is necessary — a system that offers positive outcomes for stray and feral cats.

In 2007 when we published a newsletter column, "Nothing 'Necessary' About This Evil" (see next page), we were coming to our conclusion as to exactly what the threat to cats was. We needed to find a way to explain the real issue as we understood it. It wasn't the fault either of the public or caregivers — some of whom were treated as criminals — but an outdated animal control and shelter system whose only solution to the "problem" of outdoor cats was to catch and kill them. Which was no solution at all.

Since the column's publication, entire cities and even a couple of states have rewritten their laws and ordinances, and there are hundreds of shelters that recognize feral cats as *community* cats. They are entitled to live their lives enjoying the support of groups and residents who care for them. Indeed, new ordinances embrace TNR and state that it is the law. They officially recognize cat caregivers and specifically state that such people are not the owners of feral cats for whom they care. New laws include new legal definitions that reflect the reality that there are cats who are never going to be owned or live inside a home, as well as the individuals and communities who humanely care for them.

This is the beginning of a much-needed paradigm shift in our relations with outdoor cats.

Alley Cat Action
Winter 2007
newsletter.

AlleyCatAction

A Publication of Alley Cat Allies   Celebrating 15 Years of Compassion for Feral Cats & Kittens   Winter 2007

VOLUNTEERS ACROSS AMERICA

On Any Given Sunday

On ANY GIVEN SUNDAY, MEN AND WOMEN ACROSS THE COUNTRY give up the opportunity to sleep late, eat a leisurely brunch, play golf, go shopping, or watch the latest game on TV, and instead head out to their local spay/neuter clinic to pitch in and save the lives of feral cats in their communities.

These compassionate people drive a largely underground movement that is cropping up in all kinds of communities—large and small, rural and urban—to fill the void formed when animal control services fail to adequately care for feral and stray cats. Veterinarians and veterinary technicians, the organizationally gifted who handle paperwork, and the handy volunteers who staff the grooming and surgical prep stations, all come together to create a desperately needed service.

Erin Curtis and Beth McIvor can be found one Sunday a month at the Northern Virginia No-Cost Feral Cat Spay/Neuter clinic administered by Alley Cat Allies (ACA). Erin and Beth discovered feral cats behind their house, and through them, a whole

Another happy customer of ACAs clinic observes the Sunday bustle.

Dorianne Andros looks on as Jeff Allen cradles a former feral colony member. The socialized kitten was spayed at ACAs clinic and Dorianne and Jeff adopted her on the spot.

new world. Erin says, "We realized feral cats must be everywhere in all neighborhoods and cities after we found them near our home."

At the clinic, Erin, who during the week manages web development for the federal government, helps out with surgical prep. Beth, a project manager for a software development team, does grooming. Both answered a recent call to help the clinic with trapping and brought 20 feral cats to the latest clinic. Erin says, "I believe that we are judged by how we treat our animals. I want to set an example for other people by helping animals and getting the word out about this issue. People need to know about

the work ACA does."

ACA's clinic opened its doors on October 4, 1998. Two veterinarians and three volunteers sterilized and vaccinated 10 feral cats. First envisioned by ACA National Director Becky Robinson as a way to address a critical need in the Washington, DC, area, which at the time lacked a low- or no-cost clinic, ACA's clinic has grown and evolved over the years as feral cat advocacy has evolved. The clinic now fields a crew of 40 volunteers on a Sunday and has, as of this writing, been responsible for spaying or neutering 5,800 feral cats.

Once the clinic was established word quickly spread in the Wash-

ington, DC, metro area. Soon clinic vets were sterilizing and treating as many as 100 cats in one day. Dr. Alison Mocko—who has led the clinic's volunteer vets since its inception—and her team have had great success with their implementation of juvenile spay/neuter. By practicing early-age sterilization—kittens who are at least two months old or weigh not less than two pounds—the clinic's vets have ensured that hundreds of cats did not slip through the cracks and begin reproducing simply because of their young age at the time of trapping.

Cindy Sikes, an employee of the US Customs Service during the week, does surgical prep at the clinic, checking that the cats haven't already been sterilized, clipping their fur to prepare them for surgery, and administering pain medication. After surgery, the feral cats receive their vaccinations and a general

Continued on page 7

Inside Action:

PAGE 3
In Your Backyard

PAGE 4
National Feral Cat Day 2006

PAGE 8
Feral Fact

Nothing "Necessary" About This Evil

What gets us into trouble is not what we don't know. It's what we know for sure that just ain't so. — Mark Twain

More cats are intentionally killed in the U.S. than die from any other documented cause.

Who is responsible? Surely there are not that many depraved individuals. And, in fact, there aren't. The vast majority of these killings are perpetrated not by cruel individuals, but under the authority of an antiquated animal control system. In particular, the killings are performed by government employees and government contractors, and spill over to private shelter employees. Everyone deplores this killing. Many characterize it as "evil." What separates Alley Cat Allies from many other organizations that claim it is a "necessary evil" is that ACA knows it is not.

Today's animal control system began over 100 years ago to address certain serious harms that dogs posed to humans. That system has become widespread and deeply entrenched; it is now written into all state and many local government laws, and also includes government buildings, equipment and personnel, and government contracts, budgets and revenues. The system is based on ownership of animals; it seeks to control animals by controlling their owners. The laws are a collection of owner duties to prevent damage, such as duties to leash, to muzzle, to fence, to vaccinate. But in the past three decades, the stray animal population has undergone a radical change. Cats have eclipsed dogs as the majority of the stray population, and many of these cats are not socialized to humans because they are offspring of a lost or abandoned owned animal.

Nevertheless, many animal organizations insist that the historic system based on owner liability continues to be viable today, and ignore the changed demographics of the unowned stray animal population. They claim that we need to strengthen the existing system; broaden existing laws to include cats, increase enforcement, impose more fines — in short, do more of the same. And in the interim, continue to accept that killing is a necessary evil.

But feral cats are not socialized to humans. They are not adoption candidates. To put them into an animal control system, where the only positive outcome is adoption, is to hand these animals a death sentence. For these reasons, Alley Cat Allies insists that a new animal control system is necessary — a system that offers positive outcomes for stray and feral cats. In other words, we recognize that the historic animal control system is the problem, not the solution.

Fortunately, a viable, nonlethal alternative has already been identified and is being implemented in communities across the world.

Since 1990, ACA has been the national leader in humane education about feral cats and in promoting Trap-Neuter-Return (TNR) as the only humane, effective method to reduce their population. Now you can help ACA spread the truth about the plight of feral cats. Help us reform the system of government-sanctioned killings. Together we can spread the word that the "necessary evil" of killing cats is anything but necessary.

Thank you so much for your support.

– Donna Wilcox, Board Chair

ACHIEVEMENT 16

Every Kitty — Every City
Community-Based, Life-Saving Programs

Far Right: **Feral being returned to her outdoor home after being spayed, vaccinated, and eartipped.**

In 2007 ACA launched the Every Kitty – Every City program. Our mission is to raise awareness and educate communities in targeted cities and metropolitan areas about outdoor cats, feral cat colony care, TNR, and the importance of accessible, affordable spay/neuter services through workshops, outreach, and organizing. And to change municipal ordinances as necessary.

The Every Kitty – Every City program provides individuals, groups, and veterinary professionals with the tools and basic knowledge needed to serve as a community resource. ACA rallies and assists community volunteers, local groups, veterinary clinics, and private shelters to enhance their existing TNR programs and seamlessly launch new ones.

ACA sponsors workshops, open to the public, on the best practices of TNR and colony care. ACA also recruits and trains local veterinary professionals on high-volume, low-cost spay/neuter techniques that will increase the availability of affordable services, including early-age spay/neuter and vaccination protocol.

The following locations have Every Kitty — Every City programs: Atlantic City, Baltimore, Chicago, Greater New Orleans, Washington, D.C., and Montgomery County, Maryland.

Every city is making great progress, but Baltimore is exemplary.

ACA partnered with local groups to form the Spay/Neuter Coalition for a Litter-less Baltimore. Members include local residents and humane organizations, cat colony caregivers, public health officials, and animal shelters. We worked together over a period of years to build citywide support for TNR. The coalition held monthly seminars; educated local veterinarians and worked with local animal control to provide resources and address concerns.

In 2007 the City of Baltimore enacted into law one of the country's best ordinances supporting TNR and feral cats. The ordinance serves as a model for other jurisdictions looking to define key terms more accurately and in a way that supports citizens' TNR

Every city in the program is making great progress, but Baltimore is exemplary.

efforts. The ordinance makes things better for cats, caregivers, and the community alike because it:

- Defines "feral cats" correctly as members of the species *Felis catus* (the very same species as a pet cat) who are unsocialized to humans
- Makes clear that a feral cat caregiver, although providing care to feral cats, is not the "owner" of feral cats
- Clarifies that the "return" in TNR is not abandonment
- Recognizes eartipping as a sign that a feral cat has been neutered and vaccinated against rabies
- Allows TNR to be an approved program for feral cats in the City of Baltimore

ACA will not rest until every city and county in the U.S. is cat friendly!

Model TNR Ordinance:

WHEREAS, the Board of Aldermen [or equivalent] of the [name of jurisdiction] has determined that a process of trapping, sterilizing, vaccinating for rabies, eartipping, and returning cats to their original location is an effective and humane way to manage and, over time, reduce the population of cats within the city.

NOW THEREFORE, BE IT ORDINATED BY THE BOARD OF ALDERMEN [OR EQUIVALENT] OF THE [NAME OF JURISDICTION], AS FOLLOWS:

SECTION A.

That a new Section [X] of [X] of the Municipal Code, [name of jurisdiction], is hereby enacted:
SECTION [X]: MANAGEMENT OF CAT POPULATION; PERMITTED ACTS.

A. Definitions. For purposes of this Section, the following terms shall have the following meanings:

1. "Community Cat" shall mean a cat who is abandoned, stray, lost, or feral and cared for by a community cat caregiver pursuant to this ordinance.
2. "Community Cat Caregiver" shall mean a person who, in accordance with and pursuant to a policy of Trap-Neuter-Return, provides care, including food, shelter or medical care to a community cat, while not being considered the owner, harborer, controller, or keeper of a community cat.
3. "Eartipping" shall mean the removal of the ¼ inch tip of a community cat's left ear, performed while the cat is under anesthesia, in compliance with any applicable federal or state law, and under the supervision of a licensed veterinarian, designed to identify the community cat as being sterilized and lawfully vaccinated for rabies.
4. "Trap-Neuter-Return" shall mean the process of humanely trapping, sterilizing, vaccinating for rabies, eartipping, and returning community cats to their original location.

B. Permitted Acts. The following actions shall be permitted in the City in pursuance of a process of Trap-Neuter-Return:

1. Trapping, for the sole purpose of sterilizing, vaccinating for rabies, and eartipping community cats, in compliance with any applicable federal or state law, and under the supervision of a licensed veterinarian, where applicable.
2. An eartipped cat received by local shelters will be returned to the location where trapped unless veterinary care is required. A trapped eartipped cat will be released on site unless veterinary care is required.
3. Community cat caregivers are empowered to reclaim impounded community cats without proof of ownership solely for the purpose of the implementation of the process of Trap-Neuter-Return as more particularly provided in this Section.

SECTION B.

All ordinances or parts of ordinances in conflict herewith are hereby expressly repealed.

SECTION C.

This ordinance shall be in full force and effect from and after the date of its passage.

ACHIEVEMENT 17

Clicking the Mouse
Our Online Communities Connect Thousands

Tapping the potential of social media for activism, Alley Cat Allies kicked our online presence into high gear in 2008. Through our online communities, we can now take even swifter action, mobilizing our network and reaching a broad audience to protest threats to cats as soon as harmful programs or policies are announced.

For example, when David, a 76-year-old man in Gainesville, Texas, was jailed for nine days in February 2015 for refusing to pay $900 in fines for feeding nine feral cats, we offered him support and legal assistance. We also mobilized public support for him through social media. More than 5,500 people on Facebook "liked" a report we published, and at least 1,900 people shared it. In March, we successfully lobbied, as part of a collaborative effort, for the Gainesville city council to approve a TNR ordinance by a vote of 6-1. This TNR ordinance will go a long way toward protecting and improving the lives of cats in Gainesville. We provided $15,000 in spay/neuter and vaccination funding to help launch the new program.

In New York, we published a cats' "sharegraphic" to post on social media to memorialize a horrendous cruelty case when at least 25 cats' bodies were placed in

"Killing Cats is NEVER the answer" share graphic for Alley Cat Allies' Facebook page.

Right: David, who was jailed for feeding feral cats in Gainesville, Texas.

Our most popular posts are educational in nature: winter weather tips, what to do if you find kittens outdoors, and so on.

plastic bags and hung from a tree in Yonkers. More than 8,200 caring people shared the memorial and 6,400 "liked" it.

In yet another campaign that protested a feeding ban for cats at Bayside State Prison in New Jersey, we organized a robust social media response and turned the issue around. Now, we have a great working relationship with Bayside State Prison officials and are implementing a TNR program.

Our most popular posts are educational in nature: winter weather tips, what to do if you find kittens outdoors, and so on. For example, our "Killing cats is never the answer" affirmation received more than 29,500 shares.

This and many other achievements would not have been possible without using social media. And, of course, our members and supporters working tirelessly and caring for cats everywhere.

Join FeralPower!

Sign up to receive our e-action alerts, FeralPower!, to stay up to date on urgent issues facing feral cats, such as local ordinances and legislation as well as upcoming local and national conferences, speaking engagements, and events. Go to www.alleycat.org.

Facebook
Our Facebook page is a public forum and discussion, as well as a place to share photos and swap ideas. Launched in September 2008 with 208 fans, we currently have more than 400,000. Our President and Founder, Becky Robinson, also has a page with more than 8,000 fans.
ACA: www.facebook..com/AlleyCatAllies
Becky: www.facebook.com/ACAPresident

YouTube
We have our own YouTube channel with a variety of videos, from how to humanely trap a cat (for caregivers) to a spay/neuter clinic video (for veterinarians).
www.youtube.com/user/AlleyCatAllies/featured

Twitter
Twitter is microblogging – a bit like having your own personal news service. We started with 11 followers in October 2008; we now have more than 21,000. Becky also has her own Twitter account.
ACA: www.twitter.com/AlleyCatAllies
Becky: www.twitter.com/FeralBecky

Instagram
A popular photo- and video-sharing platform. Our account was launched September 2013, and we now have more than 2,400 followers. Again, both ACA and Becky have accounts.
ACA: www.instagram.com/AlleyCatAllies
Becky: www.instagram.com/FeralBecky

ACHIEVEMENT 18

Positive Findings

Most Pet Cats Neutered

Alley Cat Allies conducted a study that was published in the *Journal of the American Veterinary Medical Association* which reports that the vast majority — at least 80 percent — of pet cats in U.S. households are neutered, with middle-to-higher-income households reporting rates of over 90 percent.

The peer-reviewed study, based on data collected for ACA by Harris Interactive and analyzed by ACA using a rigorous statistical approach, is the first nationally representative study to thoroughly examine household income as it relates to the neuter status of pet cats.

"This study indicates that spaying and neutering is an accepted, established practice among the large majority of Americans with pet cats," said Becky Robinson. "This is a very positive finding. As a result, our nation's pet cats are living much healthier lives."

The study found that family income was the strongest predictor of whether housecats are neutered. In households earning $35,000 or more annually, 93 percent of cats were neutered, compared to 51 percent of cats in households earning less than $35,000. While both income groups reported a majority of their pet cats to be neutered, the disparity underscores a challenge long observed by ACA.

Household cats represent only part of the total U.S. cat population. Previous research suggests there may be just as many stray and feral cats in the country as pet cats, and most of these cats are intact and breeding. This underscores the need for policies and programs to expand the availability of no-cost and low-cost, high-volume spay/neuter services, not only for lower-income pet owners but also for feral cats.

Based on the nationally representative sample, the study concluded that there are approximately 82.4 million pet cats in the U.S., living in a total of 36.8 million households. One third of these households reported adopting at least one of their cats as a stray. The study by K. Chu, W. M. Anderson, and M.Y. Rieser ("Population Characteristics and Neuter Status of Cats Living in Households in the United States,"

The study found that family income was the strongest predictor of whether housecats are neutered.

J Am Vet Med Assoc 2009; 234:1023-1030) consisted of 1,205 respondents across the continental U.S., contacted by telephone and selected via random-digit dial methodology. Following completion of the data collection, respondents were weighted for region, age, gender, education, income, race, and ethnicity to ensure a sample representative of the American population.

Any attempts to increase the proportion of neutered cats in the U.S. must include services for stray and feral cats.

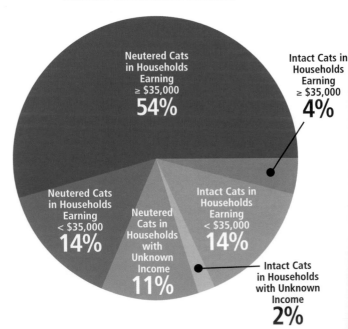

Snapshot of Neuter Status of the U.S. Pet Cat Population by Annual Household Income

Neutered Cats in Households Earning ≥ $35,000
54%

Intact Cats in Households Earning ≥ $35,000
4%

Neutered Cats in Households Earning < $35,000
14%

Neutered Cats in Households with Unknown Income
11%

Intact Cats in Households Earning < $35,000
14%

Intact Cats in Households with Unknown Income
2%

Comparison of Neuter Status for Pet Cats by Annual Household Income

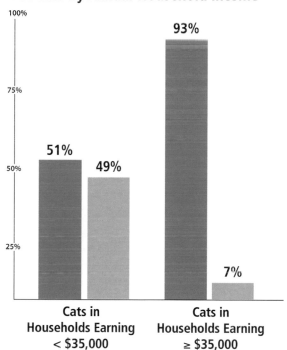

Over 90 percent of cats in households earning $35,000 or more per year were spayed or neutered, compared to 51 percent of cats in households earning less than $35,000. Further details of this study are available at www.alleycat.org.

"This study indicates that spaying and neutering is an accepted, established practice among the large majority of Americans with pet cats," said *Becky Robinson.*

■ spayed or neutered

■ not spayed or neutered (or "intact")

Spay/Neuter Status of U.S. Cat Population

Household Cats
82 Million

Stray and Feral Cats
est. 82 Million

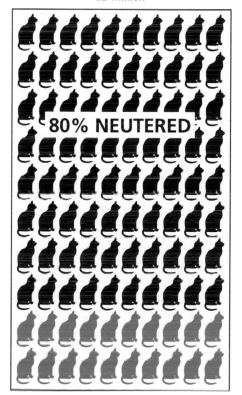

80% NEUTERED

2.3% NEUTERED

spayed or neutered

not spayed or neutered (or "intact")

ACHIEVEMENT 19

Vets are Vital

Working with Veterinarians Helps Community Cats

Veterinarians play a unique and special role in improving the lives of community cats. They are often the first people compassionate individuals turn to with questions about how to make the right choice for the cats in their care. ACA developed the Veterinary Awareness Campaign to help fill the void of information about stray and feral cats directed toward veterinarians. Drawing from more than 20 years of work with the veterinary community, the campaign delivers research, expertise, and protocols to veterinarians. ACA staff travel across the country to veterinary conferences to hand out information and promote our online Veterinary Resource Center. This is a major resource of scientific and expert information and is organized in the following sections:

- Feral Cat Health
- Feral Cat Behavior
- Feral Cat Veterinary Protocol
- Feral Cat Spay/Neuter Clinics
- Feral Cat Population
- Feral Kittens
- Trap-Neuter-Return

Dr. Alison Mocko performing spay/ neuter surgery during National Feral Cat Day 2003 clinic.

The Veterinary Resource Center includes a special section on the increasing number of scientific studies that show TNR to be a humane and effective approach for managing feral cats. The studies document how TNR improves the lives of cats and their relationships with the people who live near them, and decreases the size of colonies over time. These studies have been conducted in multiple countries and published in a variety of peer-reviewed scientific journals. For example, one study found a 66 percent decrease in the populations of managed colonies over 11 years. (Further details of this study are available at www.alleycat.org.)

By serving as a resource for the public, providing direct veterinary care, and performing the surgery portion of TNR, veterinarians help to ensure the humane treatment of community cats, who require a special veterinary approach that takes into account their unique needs and the fact that they are unsocialized to people.

Some of our outreach activities to the veterinary profession include exhibiting at the San Diego Veterinary Conference in 2009, where we spoke with veterinarians and shared our expertise.

"We received a great reception from conference attendees," said Roxana Rahmani, Programs Assistant. "We are really able to see that we are filling a void in the veterinary community by providing information about stray and feral cat care."

To help raise the issue of feral cats among veterinarians, we designed three specific ads to run in veterinary trade magazines, including *DVM, Veterinary Forum, Veterinary Technician*, and the National Association of Veterinary Technicians in America newsletter.

ACA is proud of its relationship with the veterinary community and is committed to its further positive development.

ACHIEVEMENT 20

A Conference of Cats

Architects of Change National Gathering

Some cats meow. Others are silent. Who knows whether cats are telepathic. Of course, they wouldn't want us to know. But it sure looks like it at times!

Alley Cat Allies' mission is to bring about an understanding of cats and what is in their best interests. Programs for cats are impossible to design if one lacks the knowledge about them as a species. So, bringing together top experts on all aspects of cats and kittens — their behavior, their unique abilities, their place in society, and the most effective community programs to help them — was the intention of a national conference in 2013. ACA continues to advance the discussion and create platforms so that new and improved programs are initiated and humane care becomes the norm and standard approach to handling cats.

We hosted a conference *for* cats near the nation's capital. Our motivation? The heightened momentum of new leadership for cat-specific shelter and animal control programs. Our goal? To capitalize on the knowledge of top professionals and give them a platform for sharing their expertise with advocates from around the country.

"Let's put catching and killing in the history books and file it on the shelves," declared Becky Robinson, ACA's President.

Our Architects of Change for Cats Conference in Arlington, Virginia, attracted nearly 400 attendees from 37 states, Israel, and Canada. This three-day event brought together experts and leaders from across the nation to discuss and strategize the keys to success for implementing humane programs for cats. It was also held as part of our National Feral Cat Day campaign. Special appreciation goes to the conference sponsors, Maddie's Fund and the marketing firm of Chapman Cubine Adams + Hussey.

More than two dozen animal control officers, shelter leaders, and cat advocates shared their major successes, including abolishing the failed "catch and kill" approach. Speakers noted that TNR has been

Speakers noted that TNR has been demonstrably effective in stabilizing and reducing the population of cats in their communities.

demonstrably effective in stabilizing and reducing the populations of cats in their communities. Further, it provides enormous cost savings to taxpayers because fewer healthy animals are entering shelters and being killed there.

"If you try to change the status quo, there are bound to be policymakers or leaders who misunderstand your intentions and try to block you — until you make the economic case," said Susan Cosby, then Executive Director of the Animal Care and Control Team of Philadelphia and a featured speaker at the conference. "Once they see the bottom line, they'll support you."

Other speakers included Major Steve Lamb of Spartanburg Animal Services, who said, "Our job is not to write tickets, it's to partner with the community." Lisa Tudor, founder of IndyFeral, raised a cheer when she said, "We trap in anything — even

Our Architects of Change for Cats Conference in Arlington, Virginia attracted nearly 400 advocates.

high heels and business suits. We don't care, we are going to neuter that cat." Bonney Brown, Humane Network President, wisely observed, "You have to adapt and be open-minded to save lives." Mike Arms of the Helen Woodward Animal Center in San Diego, summed it up for many when he noted, "The animals have your hearts, but it's your minds they need." John Fulton, host of Animal Planet's "Must Love Cats," entertained everyone with a series of cat-themed songs he performed.

The last word goes to Jill Kirsch of Ohio, who wrote in a Facebook post:

"Alley Cat Allies could not have put together a better conference! You showed us we are not alone in what we do and inspired us with what others are doing."

The program for the Architects of Change for Cats Conference was arranged around three primary themes: Harness your passion for cats; Expand resources for cats in your community; and Implement lifesaving shelter and animal control policies. Some of the diverse topics included:

- Common Shelter Ailments: Increasing Survival Rates through Prevention and Treatment
- Becoming an Empowered Activist: Find Your Inner Leader
- Shelters as Catalysts for Change
- Community Plans for Saving Cats
- Shelter Transformation: A Blueprint for Change
- Shelter Transformation: Expanding Lifesaving Programs for Cats
- Navigating Your Local Government: How to Discuss Cat Policies with Officials
- Common Sense for Cats: Challenging Opposition to Outdoor Cats
- Shelter Transparency
- Know Your Rights for Advocates and Caregivers
- Campaign Trail Lessons: Wake County and Camden County
- Engaging the Veterinary Community: Get Vets On Board for TNR
- Inside Animal Control
- TNR Workshops as a Catalyst for Change

Left: Special Guest Speaker John Fulton and Becky Robinson enjoy a lively conversation.

Setting the Record Straight

Challenging Dubious Research and Misinformed Media

We know that Trap-Neuter-Return works. We see the impact in countless communities across the country and in numerous methodical studies. But for the American animal control and shelter system, catching and killing outdoor cats has been the default approach for more than a century. This entrenched practice has failed. Hundreds of millions of cats have been killed in animal shelters. Scientific evidence shows that the catch-and-kill method of controlling or eliminating cats does not work. Each time cats are removed, the population rebounds through a natural phenomenon known as the "vacuum effect." New cats, either from neighboring territories or born from survivors, move in to replace their predecessors as they take advantage of the available food, water, and shelter. TNR is the only effective way to stop the reproductive cycle and stabilize and reduce populations.

The good news is that change is happening. Humane, sound, and effective programs saving animals and benefiting people are rapidly replacing outdated catch and kill. But breaking the cycle of institutional killing with TNR doesn't come easily, particularly when TNR opponents find traction for their attacks by capitalizing on the media's penchant for "scientific" research scapegoating cats as the primary threat to birds and other wildlife.

For example, in 2013 the Smithsonian Institution and the U.S. Fish and Wildlife Service funded a study that estimated domestic cats kill approximately 2.4 billion birds and 12.3 billion mammals a year. "The impact of free-ranging domestic cats on wildlife in the United States" by Scott R. Loss, Tom Will, and Peter P. Marra was published in the online journal *Nature Communications* (January 29, 2013).

Some news outlets tend to sensationalize research about outdoor cats and their environmental impact by labeling them, for example, as "serial killers." The Smithsonian study was no exception. A prominent article, "That Cuddly Kitty Is Deadlier Than You" by Natalie Angier and published in *The New York Times* (January 29, 2013), shows how exaggerated reporting frames a false conflict about outdoor cats and their impact on the environment.

These alarmist news articles leave the public confused. Cats are America's favorite pet. More cats are in people's homes than any other animal. But the general lack of understanding of community cats, combined with so many stories of cats being a threat to other animals, creates a genuine threat to outdoor cats. When a municipality is considering TNR, people's impression of outdoor cats might be based on one inflammatory news story they saw. The same also goes for opinion formers and policymakers.

This is why we analyze and review every research study. We need to be able to distinguish between sound science and hyperbole. Our job, as the voice for cats, is to set the record straight.

Leading biologists, climate scientists, and environmental watchdogs all agree that human impact on the environment is without a doubt the number one cause of species loss. Habitat destruction, pollution, and climate change are far and away the greatest threats to birds and wildlife, not cats. While this shines what can be an uncomfortable light on our behavior, sacrificing outdoor cats is pointless and cruel.

We were so disturbed by such a respected organization as the Smithsonian funding such dubious research that we commissioned our own analysis to investigate its accuracy.

Statistician Gregory J. Matthews, Ph.D., of the University of Massachusetts at Amherst, an independent researcher, conducted a thorough review of the statistics and methodology used in the study. He found major flaws, including the method used by the researchers to estimate the number of birds killed. For example, the researchers studied a small sample of cats over three summer months in one specific geographic area and extrapolated the data to cats all across the United States over all seasons. Some of the studies were decades old, including one from 1930. Matthews concluded that had he been a peer reviewer of this paper, he would have rejected it for publication. (Matthews' entire analysis can be found on our website, www.alleycat.org.)

The Smithsonian study was essentially a literature review, and not a very good one at that. The media will, of course, pay attention to research from such prestigious authorities as the Smithsonian. But the misleading conclusions and inappropriate recommendations in this study become dangerous to outdoor cats, as the media propagate them and misinform the public and fail to tell policy makers about TNR.

The only media report we saw that questioned the research was CNN's "OutFront with Erin Burnett." Burnett noted the ridiculously large margin of error the authors employed ("give or take a few billion"), deemed it "unacceptable" and told her viewers, "…when it comes to the danger of cats, it seems like they're just telling tales."

Habitat destruction, pollution, and climate change are far and away the greatest threats to birds and wildlife, not cats.

The true story is that TNR is the only effective approach for community cats. We have succeeded in educating thousands of policymakers across the country. The hundreds of new pro-TNR ordinances speak to the direction municipalities are taking.

A quarter of a century ago we set out to dismantle the outdated catch-and-kill approach — a cruel, ineffective, and wasteful policy. Our achievement is that we have succeeded — despite doubtful research and misinformed media — in making TNR the new standard of care for community cats.

Becky Robinson delivers to the Smithsonian Institution a petition signed by more than 55,000 Americans to protest a controversial study the institution funded on cats and wildlife.

Alley Cat Allies Recognized

Awards Mean Rewards for Cats

Becky Robinson receiving Lifetime Achievement Award from Jeff Dorson the Executive Director of the Humane Society of Louisiana.
Credit: Orleans Image Consulting.

Every recognition Alley Cat Allies receives for our important work for cats is a signal indicating we're making a difference to cats who are at risk through no fault of their own. Further, each award would not be possible without quite literally the allies of alley cats everywhere making a difference every day. Thank you!

2008
ACA is awarded the Friendship Key to the City of New Orleans for its animal protection efforts following Hurricanes Katrina and Rita. The same year, New Orleans was named to Alley Cat Allies'

Every Kitty — Every City program, which supports humane education and outreach efforts for caregivers and community residents.

2013
ACA is presented with the New Zealand Companion Animal Council's Assisi award in recognition of its outstanding service to animals. This is the first time that the award has been presented to an organization, instead of an individual. Bob Kerridge, patron of the New Zealand Companion Animal Council, said that ACA is being recognized for contributing "to the welfare of animals in a spectacular way."

"Alley Cat Allies…has shown the world that [community] cats can live happy and fulfilled lives through love and care," said Kerridge, who presented the award. "In New Zealand we endeavor to emulate this wonderful work, and are inspired by the organization that paved the way."

This is the first time that the award has been presented to an organization, instead of an individual.

2015
Washington Humane Society honors Becky Robinson with the Humane Hero Award as the first person to address the issue of feral cats on a national scale and introduce TNR to the American public, including in the District of Columbia.

"Starting out her efforts here in D.C. some 20-plus years ago," WHS stated, "Becky has continued to help the feral and free-roaming cat population here in the District through education, awareness and support."

Becky Robinson receives the Lifetime Achievement Award from the Humane Society of Louisiana for the work done in the Gulf region after hurricanes Katrina and Rita.

ACHIEVEMENT 23

The Future Five

A New Strategy for Cats in Shelters

Launched in 2013, ACA's Future Five: Shelter Partners to Save Cats' Lives program is helping five animal shelters adopt and expand humane programs that will save cats' lives. The selected shelters have committed to an official Feral Cat Protection Policy, which means that they will stop impounding feral cats (who are almost always killed in shelters) and instead support Trap-Neuter-Return, and only accept feral cats to divert them to TNR or Shelter-Neuter-Return programs.

When shelters stop the cycle of impounding and killing healthy feral cats, cats are protected and resources are redirected to lifesaving programs. The shelters also receive community buy-in, thereby making it easier to find volunteers, foster homes, and donors.

Each shelter receives $5,000 and one year of expert guidance from ACA. This program will not only transform these five shelters, it will also create models that shelters nationwide can follow to save even more cats' lives. Currently, there aren't many models for shelter programs for community cats that don't require

When shelters stop the cycle of impounding and killing healthy feral cats, cats are protected and resources are redirected to lifesaving programs.

significant grants. The Future Five program will fulfill the need for step-by-step blueprints for change that shelters can follow even if, like the Future Five shelters, they have limited funds and face challenges.

Management teams from each of the shelters convened in Reno, Nevada, in October 2014 for the Future Five Leadership Summit.

The Future Five
Kanawha/Charleston Humane Association (WV)

A nonprofit shelter that holds the contract for Kanawha County and multiple cities within the county, serving a population of approximately 192,000 people. In 2012, the shelter impounded 4,638 cats. Until recently, it killed most of the animals impounded. Achievements include:

- Stopped impounding and killing healthy feral cats for several cities
- Informed policymakers who now embrace TNR
- Implemented surrender-by-appointment to better serve the public and manage admissions
- Began a foster care program to socialize kittens for adoption
- Launched a new hotline service called Animal Help Desk
- Number of cats killed decreased by 90 percent in 2014 over prior year
- Nine out of 10 cats adopted or neutered, vaccinated and returned to their colony in 2014

Bay Minette City Shelter and Baldwin County Humane Society, Bay Minette (AL)

BMCS serves 8,000 residents. There is not a physical shelter. Instead, adoptable animals are boarded at two different veterinary hospitals. Between January and October 2013, the agency impounded 190 cats, and 104 were feral. Nearly all were killed. Baldwin County Humane Society is a nonprofit animal adoption agency partnering with BMCS. Achievements include:

- Stopped impounding and killing healthy feral cats as of February 2014
- Actively promotes and conducts TNR
- Initiated a new humane education program
- Distributed public educational materials
- Greatly improved relationship with the public, who now coexist with community cats

Johnson County Animal Control (IN)

A shelter that serves about 143,000 people, and in 2013 impounded 798 cats. An ordinance revised in 2013 supports TNR. The Humane Society of Johnson County is a nonprofit organization partnering with the Johnson County Animal Shelter to educate the community about TNR. Achievements include:

- Passed new TNR ordinance
- Implemented community cats program in conjunction with HSJC

- Adoption program redesigned and tripled the number of cats adopted
- New employee hired to focus exclusively on TNR
- Eight out of 10 cats adopted or neutered, vaccinated and returned to their colony in 2014

Lee County Domestic Animal Services (FL)

A government-operated shelter serving the 640,000 county residents and providing animal control services. Its average annual cat intake is about 5,000. The shelter implemented TNR in 2009. PAWS Lee County is a nonprofit organization partnering with LCDAS. It operates a spay/neuter clinic with discounts for feral cats. Achievements include:

- Implemented TNR
- The number of cats saved doubled in one year
- Became vital resource in neighborhoods providing humane education and mediation

Stanislaus Animal Services Agency (CA)

Nonprofit, volunteer run organization serving about 500,000 residents that used to impound 18,000–19,000 animals each year. In 2012, it impounded 7,948 cats and kittens and its live release rate for cats was 7 percent. In 2013, SASA partnered with the Humane Society of Stanislaus County to start community-supported TNR. Achievements include:

- Created a TNR program in conjunction with the HSSC and the Cat Network of Stanislaus
- Increased adoption outreach and marketing to reach broader public base
- Seven out of 10 cats adopted or neutered, vaccinated, and returned to their colony in 2014

ACHIEVEMENT 24

Popular with the People

Humane Government Programs Wanted

"An informed citizenry is at the heart of a dynamic democracy," said Thomas Jefferson, third president of the United States and author of the Declaration of Independence.

While he may not have had cats foremost in his mind, we take very seriously Jefferson's intent by representing the interests of cats and their moral and legal status and, when appropriate, using the First Amendment in the Bill of Rights to petition the government.

Alley Cat Allies works hard to end the killing of cats and promote their humane care with education, training, advocacy, and building relationships to help people make a difference for the cats in their community. Caring for cats is not only the

Setting a standard of well-being for the entire species based on the life of indoor cats ignores the true habitat and natural history of cats.

responsibility of compassionate people, but also engaged governments.

In the past quarter century we have made significant progress for cats in advocacy, public opinion and public policy, but there's still much work to be done.

In 2007 we commissioned Harris Interactive to conduct a nationally representative survey of public attitudes toward the humane treatment of stray cats. The survey revealed that an overwhelming majority of Americans — 81 percent — believe that leaving a stray cat outside to live out his or her life is more humane than having the cat caught and killed. (See "U.S. Public Opinion on Humane Treatment of Stray Cats" by Karyen Chu, Ph.D., and Wendy M. Anderson, J.D., at www.alleycat.org.)

This finding reveals a significant disparity between the public's humane ethic and the operating policy of most U.S. animal pounds and shelters: that it is more humane to kill stray cats than to let them live out their lives outdoors. The catch-and-kill policy rests on

untenable bases; a policy that promotes "euthanasia" of stray cats as being in the cats' best interests is at odds not only with the humane values of most Americans, but also with pounds and shelters as part of a humane movement, unnecessarily killing the clients they were founded to serve.

The animal control and shelter system erroneously paints cats as a species that only belongs indoors and in human households. This is contrary to the natural history of *Felis catus*, a species that has flourished outdoors for thousands of years. Setting a standard of well-being for the entire species based on the life of indoor cats ignores the true habitat and natural history of cats. The animal control and shelter system, which claims cats are better off dead than alive outdoors, acts in direct opposition to the scientific research that indicates feral cats lead good lives, and to the beliefs of the general public about what is the humane treatment of cats.

In the same year as our survey, we published a column in our newsletter, *Alley Cat Action*, called "Nothing 'Necessary' About This Evil," which challenged the animal control and shelter system and its outdated catch-and-kill policy. (See Achievement 15: Nothing "Necessary" About This Evil)

As we worked with many individuals and organizations across the country, and empowered many more to implement TNR and other lifesaving programs in their communities, we also called for a paradigm shift in attitudes and ideas, and the need for systemic public policy change for cats. We showed that vaccinated and spayed cats in colonies can live well, and the animal control and shelter system should substantially reform its policies by stopping the killing and embracing TNR and other nonlethal methods.

As we look forward to the next 25 years of advocacy, we welcome the increasing numbers of individuals and organizations who share our understanding of the importance of TNR as the only effective, safe, and humane way to help and stabilize community cat populations. Trap-Neuter-Return is endorsed by local governments ranging from conservative Colorado Springs, Colorado, to liberal Berkeley, California, and by our nation's capital, Washington, D.C., and Baltimore, Maryland. Because TNR decreases the size of cat colonies, improves public health, and is humane and economical, it is an appealing method of care for many different interest groups and organizations, not all of them related to animal protection.

We also welcome as supporters of TNR such organizations as The Humane Society of the United States and such experts as veterinarian Kate Hurley, formerly an animal control officer at the Santa Cruz (CA) SPCA and currently the Program Director for the Koret Shelter Medicine Program at the University of California-Davis School of Veterinary Medicine. She wrote ("For Community Cats, A Change is Gonna Come" in *Animal Sheltering* Sep/Oct 2013):

"Acknowledging the failures of a system in which so much has been invested may be initially discouraging, but it opens the door to consideration of new possibilities. Knowing that euthanasia [sic] of healthy cats neither controls feline populations nor protects individual cats, there is freedom in realizing how little we have to lose."

She concluded with this heartfelt plea:

"Then I imagine we just stop. We don't admit one more healthy cat to a shelter than we can release alive. And I imagine that enormous river of resources and compassion diverted to finding other solutions, to spay/neuter services, to educating the public, to caring for domestic and wild animals, to finding ways to protect all the species we treasure. I imagine you, reading this article. I wonder what your role is and what it would mean to you if we could see a day when no healthy cat was euthanized in our shelters. I hope we don't have to wait another 20 years to find out."

Throughout ACA's work, we show how we fulfill our mission to transform and develop communities to protect and improve the lives of cats. We also speak about the opposition to TNR we received from some organizations in the animal protection movement. In the 25 years since our founding, eight years since the Harris Interactive survey, and the publication of our challenge to the traditional shelter system, Alley Cat Allies is making a difference. But the well-being of cats should be more than just our responsibility. Perhaps our biggest achievement is that we have positively influenced many in the animal control and shelter system, as well as more broadly in the animal protection movement and in society in general.

"The past is personal at ACA because our organization was born from the unexpected encounter of a feral cat colony in a Washington, D.C., neighborhood," said Becky Robinson. "Our future must be also personal as we recommit ourselves to resolving the issues of all cats in our lives — those who live with us and those who live around us — by educating people and lobbying governments to be wise and effective. Truth, compassion, and nonviolence is the way forward for all concerned."

Team Feline

Our Office is Their Home

Right hand page:
First column top: **Oliver.**
Bottom: **Charles.**
2nd column top: **Diana.**
Bottom: **Fergie.**

Cats live, work, and play in our headquarters. They remind us everyday of the reasons why we're committed to the cause of protecting and improving the lives of cats. People light up when they arrive and see Oliver lounging on the reception counter. "How do you get any work done?" they ask. The cats are truly a perk at Alley Cat Allies.

Every cat in the office forms a unique bond with the staff. They enrich our work and lives every day. They help us write by sitting on or near our keyboards. They lead our meetings from lying in the center of the conference room table. They keep us on task with a gentle nudge of their paw.

Our first headquarters cats were Jared, Jazzy, and Coo. There will always be a soft spot in our hearts for Coo, a charmer who wooed everyone he met. He was patient, sweet, deaf, and FIV-positive. Loving him reminded us of the importance of FIV education. FIV wasn't a death sentence for Coo, who loved life and lived happily and safely along with our FIV-negative cats for 10 years. Jared — "King of the Office" — was confident and demanding in the most endearing way. If he wanted something, he'd stand on his back legs and tap you on the arm. No one could visit the office without Jared checking them out. We'll never forget him. Jazzy had a loud personality — literally. Jazzy strutted down the office halls meowing loud enough to make staff take breaks from their work to pet her. She was our resident love-bug. We miss her deeply.

Our office has also been a halfway house for dozens of foster cats who are now in loving homes. Some of the more notable among them include a litter of six "cow" (as in Holstein-colored) kittens and Cody. Their white-with-black markings were just like those of Holstein cows. The cow kittens were trapped together in Arlington, Virginia within a few minutes of each other. They were fostered for three weeks and all of us were smitten with them. We held meetings on the floor in their private foster room. They were adopted in pairs by the best homes in the world.

Cody was trapped in Laurel, Maryland by our then special projects manager, Amanda Novotny, in 2013

along with his siblings and their mom. Cody's foster dad (and later adoptive dad), our then office manager, Ron Erickson, brought him to work every day for weeks and we fell in love. He became known as "The Coders 'round these parts." Cody needed a lot of tender loving care, as he was very underweight and sickly. Now, he's healthy and enjoys life with his two older feline brothers — also office foster graduates!

Every cat in the office forms a unique bond with the staff.

Every cat we've helped in the last 25 years is an achievement that wouldn't have been possible without the thousands of individuals and hundreds of organizations throughout the U.S. who work toward achieving our mission to "transform and develop communities to protect and improve the lives of cats."

Team Feline Today

Currently, there are four cats who live in the office. They are Oliver and "the Royals:" Charles, Diana, and Fergie. Their main caregiver is Donna Wilcox, our vice president. Her desk is one big cat bed. They spend a lot of time in her office.

Oliver, aka, "The Dapper Gentleman" (b. April 2009) The Shredder

Oliver came to us through ACAs' Every Kitty – Every City program. Our Atlantic City Field Work Coordinator, found him wandering near the boardwalk. She realized he was a socialized cat. She put him into foster care and began searching for a permanent home. It didn't take long before we realized that the perfect home was right under our noses. Although Oliver is content to entertain himself by shredding papers found on desks, chasing paperclips, feathers, and other distractions up and

down the hall, our furry friend has already bonded with Charles. His days are enriched by both human and feline companions.

most ladylike postures with her front paws neatly crossed. She is also the most playful, always ready for a session with the laser pointer. She can entertain herself with a paperclip, batting it throughout the halls. When we first moved into our Bethesda, Maryland, office, it took her a week before she came out of the supply closet. She also disappeared into the ceiling for a few hours and did that a few times before we were able to discover how she was getting up there and blocked her access.

Charles, aka, "Chuck" (b. May 2002)
File Clerk

Charles, Fergie, and Diana were trapped together from a colony in southeast Washington, D.C., at about three months of age. Charles is a truly regal looking cat with long slender legs and a lean muscular body. He is quite the lover, giving head-butts, sitting on laps, and rolling on his back for tummy rubs. He has a snaggle tooth and can often be found with his tongue sticking out slightly. He likes to tip over glasses of water – many papers have been drenched with his help. He loves to chew on string and rubber bands, so they must be kept out of his reach. One of his favorite occupations is jumping into filing cabinet drawers and "helping" to alphabetize folders. Charles can be a fair-weather friend, favoring one staff member for a couple of months, then moving on to another.

Diana, aka, "Princess Diana" (b. May 2002)
Etiquette Officer

Diana, who is now 13, remains the shyest of all our office cats. She loves getting attention and being petted. But it has to be on her terms. She sits in the

Fergie, aka, "Fergie-Bergie" (b. May 2002)
Party Planner

Fergie is Diana's sister, and was trapped in southeast Washington, D.C., at the age of 10 weeks. Diana and Fergie were trapped at the same time and were the same age. Fergie is our smallest cat. Her meow is a little squeak. She likes to use people to get from one place to another, treating them like just another piece of furniture. She can be forceful when ready to be petted, and will give a little nip to make sure we are paying attention. She is very slender, but has a belly that hangs low and flops from side to side when she runs down the hall. She'll come around with a look of "Whatcha up to? Wanna play?"

Cat Chat

Rethinking Our Relationship with Cats

President Becky Robinson and Vice President Donna Wilcox reflect upon changing attitudes toward cats as Alley Cat Allies was forming in 1990, and today after a quarter century of cat advocacy. They sat down together recently at the organization's headquarters in Bethesda, Maryland, and had a conversation looking back over 25 years of advocacy for cats.

BECKY ROBINSON: Organizations like Alley Cat Allies start because there's a story. Ours began when I walked down an alleyway and discovered a feral cat colony. Soon, others wanted to join together to help the colony. We could have just helped a few cats and left. But we saw there was a bigger need.

DONNA WILCOX: Cats were becoming more popular but there was little information about their behavior or needs. Not just feral cats but all cats. If you took your cat to the vet, maybe the vet knew some

As we all know, when you get your first cat, that's it. You fall in love with them.

things about cat medicine because they studied it a little. But their primary focus was dogs. They knew very little about cat behavior. And there were a lot of different diseases that only cats get (e.g., FeLV, FIV, FIP). Cats were mostly killed in shelters. They didn't know how to treat cats. Shelters were designed and built to house dogs, not cats.

BECKY: People called us and were upset because their shelter didn't help (feral) cats.

DONNA: We began to get calls in our homes after we started. We didn't have an office then. As soon as people found out we existed, we were flooded with requests for advice and assistance. People were

Becky Robinson and Donna Wilcox holding the Humane Hero Award presented to Alley Cat Allies in 2015.

desperate. People didn't want the cats they were caring for to be killed by animal services. They didn't know what to do because they couldn't touch them. How are they going to get them to the vet to spay or neuter? If they could find a vet willing to help. How do I catch this cat? I can't touch her or pick her up and put her in a carrier. They didn't know about humane traps, much less how to trap.

BECKY: I remember a lot of stories where people called their vets and they wouldn't help them. A few courageous people told us they had longstanding relationships with their vets and sort of gave them ultimatums because they needed the vet's help: "I've been coming here with my cat and dog for 20 years. You're going to help me with this stray."

DONNA: I got my first cat when I was 20 or 21. I was living with my parents at the time. I had grown up with dogs and was a dog person and had dogs at the time. But my boss's Siamese cat had kittens, and she asked if I would like one. So I took one of them. As we all know, when you get your first cat, that's it. You fall in love with them. They take over your lives. I became a ferocious reader of anything I could get my hands on about cats — books, magazines — and there wasn't much around then.

My first cat stayed with my parents when I moved out because he had become the family cat. Then I got another cat, Zero, but having primarily had dogs in the past, I treated this cat the way you would treat a dog. I never had a carrier for him. I took him everywhere with me. I had a leash and collar for him. Back in those days, there were no laws against taking cats anywhere. So I used to take him to the grocery store and to [department stores] Hecht's and Woodies. We traveled in the car without a carrier; he'd just sit in the passenger seat. And I took him for walks. He would just follow along. I treated him like a dog because I didn't know any better. When I think back, though, I could have lost him by not knowing how cats react to strange situations.

BECKY: You worked at the Natural Resources Defense Council for 22 years. And you had a wall in your office with pictures of your colleagues' cats. You knew the names of all the cats and their story.

DONNA: NRDC people knew I was interested in cats. They asked me questions, which I answered, and, by word of mouth, I would get calls from colleagues from across the country, mostly about behavioral problems.

BECKY: What were the questions people asked you?

DONNA: Oh, it ran the gamut. The same kinds of questions that we have now. Why is my cat not using the litter box? That was always, even back then, the number one. Things they didn't like or things they didn't understand. Jumping up on the counter. Scratching the furniture. Some said they couldn't get their cats to the vet. They didn't know how to get them into the carrier because the cat would be scared and would scratch them.

And for a long time, the big national organizations that were animal rights and animal welfare completely ignored cats.

BECKY: So by the time we started Alley Cat Allies, were there more dogs in homes than cats, but cats were becoming increasingly popular?

DONNA: Yes, I think a majority of people who had dogs only had one dog. But most people who had cats had two or more. So, you would have more cats in households but not necessarily more people with cats than dogs. I think the reason was because people's lifestyles were changing. That was why I got my cat. I had dogs but I was moving into an apartment with a roommate. We were both going to be at work from 7:30 a.m. to 5:30 or 6 p.m. You can't leave a dog in an apartment for that long.

BECKY: A cat was better for busier people working longer hours.

DONNA: Because they could use the litter box.

BECKY: But there was no one to turn to for help. Not the shelters. Vets didn't know much about cats. And they wouldn't treat feral cats at all. They didn't know how to handle them since they were not tame.

DONNA: Sometimes people would get misinformation from the vets.

BECKY: Well, even about your housecats —

DONNA: With my second cat, the vet recommended I

Panda, the first feral kitten Donna Wilcox adopted and socialized.

Sidwell Friends
students enjoying
their internship
with Alley Cat Allies
in 2000.

have him declawed. Of course I didn't, thank goodness.

BECKY: How did you know not to do that? How did you say no?

DONNA: It just didn't seem right.

BECKY: Oh, I'm not going to do that to him. So for some people, it's common sense, but you're right. This shows the limited understanding of cats at the time regarding even socialized cats. As we've said about feral cats, even when someone did know how to trap a feral cat with a humane box trap and get her to a vet, the veterinary staff were not set up to handle them. Many mistakes were made.

DONNA: My first feral cat, Panda, was before Alley Cat Allies. In 1990, I had read an article about AnnaBell Washburn and Trap-Neuter-Return in *Cat Fancy* (by Ellen Perry Berkeley) and that's how I trapped Panda. I called the Washington Humane Society to get a trap. They told me that they would give me a trap, but I had to return it with the cat if I trapped one. So I got a trap from them and caught Panda, the cat I found in a construction area. WHS said that if I brought her in they would euthanize her because they wouldn't be able to find a home for her since she's feral. And I said, "Well, what if I tame her?" and they said, "Well, if she's tame, we'll try to find a home for her." But of course when I got her, I took the trap back

to them because I had to, but I also told them I had never trapped a cat.

BECKY: That was the case in many jurisdictions when we started. That if they loan you a trap, you have to bring it back with the cat. There are hundreds of jurisdictions that still have the same old policies.

DONNA: Yes. Panda was eight months old when I got her and I couldn't touch her. She lived to be 12 and became socialized so I could touch her, but only on her terms.

BECKY: So, people found us and were begging for answers. They wanted to learn about TNR because they didn't want kittens born.

DONNA: Right. And they didn't want the cats injured. And for a long time, the big national organizations that were animal rights and animal welfare completely ignored cats. It was almost like they didn't exist. You could save the gorillas and the whales but not feral cats. It's perfectly okay for them to be killed in the shelters, and —

BECKY: — And that was considered humane. Yet we had all these humane programs to save the whales and save the elephants, but we should kill cats.

DONNA: There were many animal conferences. We all attended them. But you, more than anybody else, ended up debating the heads of these groups about TNR and feral cats. And the interesting thing was that after three or four years, you finally said, "I'm not debating this anymore." You said, "If you want me to come and talk about feral cats and TNR, I'll do that, but I'm not debating it."

BECKY: So, there was no national organization advocating for cats. Nobody was standing up for them. *Cat Fancy* magazine wrote about them, but obviously they weren't an advocacy group.

DONNA: I think the main thing we've done from the very beginning — and still do — is advocate for cats. We have really stood behind our conviction that TNR is the method to use — we don't just back down in the face of opposition and concede, as some have suggested, that TNR is only okay under certain, limited circumstances.

BECKY: Right. "And you can kill some."

DONNA: Or if the homeowner doesn't want them, then you have to relocate or kill them. If one of them has some disease, you have to kill them all. We don't support any of that. All we say is true advocacy for the cat. Even if you came across a colony that looks perfectly healthy and there is no caregiver, it's still better to TNR them and leave them be. That's come to be known as Feral Freedom programs in some communities.

BECKY: If you can't get them to the vet or whatever, just leave them alone.

DONNA: Right. We've never felt that we have the right to kill an animal, a healthy animal.

BECKY: This movement is now huge. There are hundreds upon hundreds of TNR organizations. Some are very small with two people that have helped perhaps a hundred cats. Others are huge, citywide, that have helped thousands of cats. And as with any movement, everybody takes their position, including what they're willing to do, what their guidelines are, what is acceptable about returning cats to an area with or without a caregiver. We try to figure out where the sticking points are and resolve them.

DONNA: Different groups take different stands on what they feel is a healthy cat. For example, there are some that still test for FeLV and FIV — and then if a cat tests positive, which may not even be truly positive — then they say they have to be killed rather than put back out, which we do not say.

BECKY: It was important for us to have a greater understanding of the science, the medicine, what the options were. Recently, a caregiver brought in a very, very sick cat. The caregiver was upset and wanted the cat to be brought back. They had discussed euthanizing the cat. "Is this cat suffering? Is there nothing that can be done?" I asked. "No. The veterinarian says nothing can be done," I was told. "We have to make the decision that's in the best interest of the cat," I replied. The manager here of that program had the cat transferred to a specialist. The cat was treated and is fine now and returned to the caregiver. We keep pushing for what is the right thing for the cat.

DONNA: Another thing is that we've had vets who won't do early-age spay/neuter, which is very important. You know, it's what's known as "juvenile" spay/neuter. It's essential for cats. They can get pregnant so young. Then we had vets in the early days who wouldn't eartip.

BECKY: Eartipping is a big one.

DONNA: It's a big one because it saves lives.

BECKY: Some of them wouldn't vaccinate against distemper. That was a problem. They wouldn't give them painkillers. But that was then…

DONNA: The point of this is that at every level, we've tried to learn as much as we can and promote best practices so that cats live out their lives in the way they're meant to. I follow a group online doing a huge TNR program. They've got over 200 cats in one location, and they've done a lot of them. But they carry

Alley Cat Allies' mascot, Frank the Feral®, sports his own tee shirt with social network tag #FrankTheFeral.

Becky Robinson with Roger Tabor, biologist and cat expert, who studied the feral cats who lived in London's Fitzroy Square in the 1970s. Also the home of the cats who were the muses for T.S. Eliot's *Old Possum's Book of Practical Cats*, the inspiration for the musical *Cats*. Trap-Neuter-Return carried out in the 70s has worked and no feral cats are in Fitzroy Square today."

it even one step further than we do. If a cat is pregnant, they wait on TNR until she has had the kittens.

BECKY: But speaking of that, there are some really difficult parts to this.

DONNA: But we tell people what we feel the best practice is. Spaying a pregnant female or bringing her in and letting her have the kittens is an example. We give them all the information we have — how stressful it is for a feral cat to be confined while she gives birth; know that you can't assist her if she has trouble while she's giving birth; confining her until the kittens are old enough to be taken away; getting her spayed — to spaying her while she's pregnant and returning her. We tell them the whole gamut. Then we say, "It's your decision because you are the caregiver." We do not say, "You have to do this."

BECKY: You have to empower people with information about the different scenarios.

DONNA: They are giving their heart and soul to these animals. You can't make them feel guilty —

BECKY: That's right.

DONNA: — because they've contacted you and you want them to do their best and get the best information. But, ultimately, it's their decision.

BECKY: We say, "Let's give you the information" and "This is what's going to happen."

DONNA: Right.

BECKY: And we have to explain to them the reality and the consequences of what they may do. A lot of people still think that kittens taken to a shelter will be adopted. At many shelters, they won't be.

DONNA: What we found was when someone called us who was concerned about the cats, but wanted them gone, is that when we gave them the information about what will happen to them if they're removed, they often said, "No. I don't want the cats hurt." So, I think one of the more brilliant things you ever came up with was DC CAT.

BECKY: DC CAT changed the landscape for the Washington, D.C., metropolitan area. Now we are working with Montgomery County. And, towns like Laurel and Bowie in Prince George's. But we just couldn't be in the nation's capital and not make a difference for cats here. You just have to stop and say, "Enough is enough. We've got to change this."

Glossary

Campus Cat
A community cat who lives on a college or university campus.

Cat Colony
A family group of community or feral cats. A group of cats who congregate, more or less, together as a unit and share a common food and shelter source.

Community Cat
Domestic cats who make their home outdoors. Most community cats are feral and not socialized to people. Community cats have different levels of socialization, from friendly to feral. Although some community cats may be social with people, they are almost always killed when taken to shelters. This is why it is best for them to remain in their outdoor home with their family colony.

Domestic Cat
Refers to the species *Felis catus* or *Felis silvestris catus*. Whether in a home or in a cat colony, cats are all the same species. The domestic cat came into existence about 10,000 years ago when humans began farming. According to scientists, cats are the only animal who domesticated themselves — choosing to live near humans to feed on the rodents attracted by stored grain. Evolutionary research shows that the natural habitat of cats is outdoors in close proximity to humans. After the invention of cat litter in the 1940s, more owned cats were kept solely indoors.

Eartip
The universal symbol and the best identifier for a community cat as being in a TNR program. In surgery, approximately 3/8 of an inch is cut off the tip of the cat's left ear in a straight line, while the cat is anesthetized. In some locations and programs, the eartip is on the right ear. An eartip can be seen from a distance, unlike a tattoo, and does not endanger a cat like a collar could.

Euthanize
Genuine euthanasia is a medical decision to end the life of a terminally ill or untreatably injured animal. Most cats who end up in shelters are killed, not euthanized. Using the word "euthanasia" is misleading, and masks what really happens to cats in pounds and shelters.

Feral or Community Cat Caregiver
Any person who provides volunteer care to a cat living outdoors. A caregiver, although providing care to cats, is not the "owner" of the cats. Community cats sometimes become accustomed to their caregivers, but not socialized for placement in homes.

Feral Cat
Domestic cats who are not socialized to people and are unowned. Feral cats typically avoid contact with humans. They are not likely to ever become lap cats or enjoy living indoors, and are therefore not adoptable and do not belong in shelters. Feral kittens can be socialized at an early age and adopted into homes. Also called alley cats, barn cats, tomcats, outdoor cats, and street cats.

Feral Cat Problem
You may see this phrase in news articles, but feral or community cats are not the "problem." People may have concerns about feral cats, and a community may need TNR to stabilize their cat populations, but calling the cats a "problem" only demonizes them. Instead, address concerns and discuss humane approaches to cat populations. The lack of TNR programs in every community is the problem.

No-Kill
A philosophy of animal sheltering where each animal is considered as an individual and where animals are only euthanized for serious medical issues where there is little hope of restoring quality of life through treatments or management of a condition or for public safety (e.g., dangerously aggressive dogs). A community is generally considered to be no-kill when at least 90 percent of all animals arriving at shelters are saved – adopted or placed in TNR programs if they are community cats. Some communities have exceeded this 90 percent benchmark. TNR is a crucial component of creating no-kill communities. There is no single universally accepted definition of the term no-kill, nor a precise standard or set of policies adhered to by all shelters using the no-kill label. There is no legal definition for no-kill.

Rehabilitate
Feral cats are not damaged and it is not our goal to make them all friendly pet cats. While it is not unheard of for

someone to socialize a feral cat, it requires a great deal of time that could be spent doing TNR for more cats. Try using "socialize" instead.

Socialized Cat

A domestic cat who is socialized and friendly with people; can be adopted into a home. Commonly known as a "pet cat." The terms "socialized cat" and "household cat" are interchangeable.

Stray Cat

A cat who has been socialized to people at some point in her life, but has left or lost her indoor home. She may become feral as her contact with humans dwindles. She can, under the right circumstances, become a pet cat once again. Stray cats who are re-introduced to a home after living outdoors may require a period of time to re-acclimate, as they may be frightened and wary after spending time outside away from people.

TNR Ordinance

A Trap-Neuter-Return law made by a city, town, or other local government that addresses the spaying and neutering of community cats. TNR ordinances can be beneficial. It is important to note that an ordinance is not necessary for an individual or an organization to practice TNR. Ordinances that are restrictive or require registration of colonies or caregivers can be detrimental to cats.

Transparency and Transparency Laws

Transparency is when animal shelters record and report all animal data that show, at a minimum, all incoming animals regardless of age, health or temperament, and the outcome for all animals (adoption, returned to owner, returned to field, transferred, killed/euthanasia, etc.). The majority of states do not mandate record keeping and reporting. Many shelters do not even record such basic information as intake and euthanasia rates. Transparency is essential to transforming America's animal control and shelter system and ending the killing of healthy, treatable animals. Alley Cat Allies advocates for all 50 states to legislatively mandate record keeping and public reporting for all animal shelters and pounds.

Trap-Neuter-Return (TNR)

A nonlethal approach to cat population control where community/feral cats are humanely trapped, sterilized and vaccinated, eartipped, and then returned to the location where they were originally trapped. Socialized cats and kittens can be adopted into homes. TNR stabilizes the colony's population and eventually reduces the number to zero. Also known as Return to Field (RTF) or Shelter-Neuter-Return (SNR). TNR is the humane, effective answer to discredited catch and kill policies, which are cruel and ineffective.

Vacuum Effect

One of many reasons why catch and kill programs are ineffective and futile. Removing cats may temporarily reduce the number of cats in an area, but two things happen: intact survivors move in to take advantage of existing resources and breed to capacity. This is a phenomenon known as the vacuum effect and is documented worldwide.

Wild

All cats are domestic cats. When describing unsocialized outdoor cats, use "feral" or "community" instead of "wild". "Feral" more accurately describes a cat's place on the spectrum of socialization. Calling a cat "wild" is confusing and leads people to believe outdoor cats are a different species than friendly pet cats. They are not.

Our Wish List for Cats

Here's to the Next 25 Years

Whether they live inside our homes or outside in our neighborhoods, cats are important to us. They're unique and special creatures who deserve, regardless of their circumstances, the best from us. Alley Cat Allies is committed to transforming and developing communities to protect and improve the lives of cats. Our mission is integral to our vision of a society in which people value and safeguard the lives of animals. Americans are coming together to make a big difference to the lives of community cats.

Trap-Neuter-Return is increasingly understood by people and their elected representatives as the only humane and effective way to care for outdoor cats. Our single greatest achievement in our first 25 years was to make TNR mainstream. As we move forward for our second quarter century of cat advocacy, we want to share with you our wish list for cats. Everyone has a role to play. Please get in touch with your ideas about our wish list.

A revolution is underway across America. A paradigm shift in our relationship with animals sweeps across the country. Out goes the old thinking of animals as "things" of no value or importance. In comes the new way to view animals as sentient beings with whom we're lucky to share our lives.

- The animal control and shelter system is transformed to a network of rescue centers and sanctuaries with hubs for all services, humane and compassionate, for at risk and homeless animals.
- Animal care facilities only euthanize cats when it is a medical decision, and it is always done in an individual animal's best interest.
- Cats live in a society that legally and morally recognizes their intrinsic worth as individual sentient beings with their own unique personalities, and their history and place in nature.
- Every public and private organization in the animal control and shelter system embraces and practices TNR.
- Cat wellness clinics throughout America

significantly contribute to the health and welfare of cats by offering free and low-cost veterinary services including TNR, spaying/neutering, vaccination, health checks, microchipping, flea treatment, etc.
- Cats, along with all other animals included in state anti-cruelty statutes, receive the full protection of the law and its enforcement.
- TNR is understood by the public and recognized in public policy as the principal safe, humane, and effective method of population control for cats.
- State-coordinated programs require transparency in the animal control and shelter system, including public and private facilities, by gathering and making publicly available data on the cats in their care.
- State governments and local municipalities recognize cat colony caregivers as legitimate animal advocates engaged in a valued public service.
- The federal government recognizes Alley Cat Allies as the innovator in TNR and consults with them on the implementation of TNR at their facilities.
- Alley Cat Allies advises public and private organizations in the animal control and shelter system, when they are awarded contracts with state and local government agencies, to implement TNR at their facilities.
- Professional organizations such as the American Veterinary Medical Association unreservedly embrace TNR and incentivize their members to offer free and low-cost spay/neuter services for all cats.
- Effective and safe non-surgical sterilization methods for cats are developed and implemented in order to improve their lives, and are in their best interest medically and legally.
- The United Nations recognizes Alley Cat Allies as the innovative organization in cat care and empowers us to reach countries throughout the world with our life saving programs for cats.

ABOUT

About Alley Cat Allies

Alley Cat Allies is the innovator in the protection and humane treatment of cats. As the only national advocacy organization dedicated exclusively to cats, ACA has worked for 25 years to support caregivers, change laws, improve shelters, and most importantly, save cats. Since our founding in 1990, we have popularized Trap-Neuter-Return (TNR) as the only humane and effective approach to community cats. By establishing and promoting standards of care, our organization has brought humane treatment of cats into the national spotlight. Before Alley Cat Allies, TNR was virtually unknown in America, and no local governments supported it. Today, a growing list of more than 500 municipalities officially embrace TNR.

Today, with more than 500,000 supporters, ACA leads the movement to protect cats' lives. We promote humane, sound policies for cats in communities all over America. We work toward a world that values the lives of all animals. Our 25 years of experience in grassroots organizing, hands-on activism, advocacy, and education empowers policymakers, veterinarians, nonprofit and volunteer groups, activists, and caregivers. We make available the tools and knowledge to practice, teach, and advocate for humane care for cats. From our headquarters in Bethesda, Maryland, our staff of more than 30 provides the national voice for cats and the millions of Americans who value cats.

Vision
A society in which people value and safeguard the lives of animals.

Mission
To transform and develop communities to protect and improve the lives of cats.

Values
- We value the intrinsic dignity and worth of each cat, and acknowledge their history and place in the natural landscape.
- We value the relationship between people, the earth, and all animals, and acknowledge that the inherent interests of all sentient beings must be given equal consideration.
- We value people and their compassion for cats.
- We value actions that advance cats' best interests.
- We value teamwork as a means to achieve common goals.
- We value learning as a means to guide our work to protect and improve the lives of cats.
- We value our right as Americans to organize and speak freely.